ONCE by the PACIFIC

Copyright © 2012 by Sarah Koops Vanderveen and Brooks Street Books, Laguna Beach.

All photographs copyright © 2012 Sarah Koops Vanderveen

All rights reserved.

No part of this book may be reproduced in any form without written permission from the publisher.

For information about other titles by Brooks Street Books, please see www.brooksstreetbooks.com

Cover and interior designed by Allison Tosti

Printed in China

ISBN 978-0-615-55653-6

ONCE by the PACIFIC

Laguna Beach in Poems and Pictures

SARAH KOOPS VANDERVEEN

FOR **DAVID, SCHUYLER & WILLEM**

A NOTE FROM THE AUTHOR

Once upon a time, I was a young girl whose father would read poetry to her and her sister and brothers before bedtime. Some were poems about mythical creatures like goblins and nymphs. Others were about everyday events, a train at a railroad crossing or lapping lake water. The rhythms, images, and sounds of those poems—the way a poet could convey an experience vividly or tell a story in so few words—stayed with me.

Many years later, after I moved to Laguna Beach with my husband and sons, I began to write poetry myself. As a daily discipline, I decided to write a poem a day for a year, and also took pictures and posted them to my blog, which I called Once by the Pacific, after the Robert Frost poem. I found that writing poetry gave me a reason to pay closer attention to the world around me.

And why poems and pictures of Laguna Beach? I love my community and sometimes can't believe I get to live here. I am inspired daily by the beauty of the Pacific Ocean and by the beautiful spirits of the people I get to call friends and neighbors. Those are the things I find myself writing about the most. How could I not be moved by the buzz of excitement in town when a south swell arrives and almost everyone I know is checking the surf at Brooks Street? Or the hot-orange color of aloe in bloom in Heisler Park? Or the loveliness of layers of ten million year-old fossilized rock at Crystal Cove?

At the end of my year of writing poems, I realized that I had enough poems and pictures of Laguna Beach to fill a book, which is what you now hold in your hands.

—Sarah Koops Vanderveen

CONTENTS

West Swell 13

Catalina Island After the Rain 14

Open and Shut 17

Cowboy, Rest in Peace 19

In Memory of Rick Griffin, Surely an
Honorary Lagunan if Ever There Was One 22

Friday Night Lights 24

Brooks Street After the Rain 27

Del Mar Avenue 31

Heisler Park in Winter 33

All Things New 34

Hike 37

Mustard 39

Canyon 41

Sea 47

A Good Morning 49

Spring Break 50

Hakama Glory Day 52

Heisler Park in Spring	55
Green Glass	56
Day's End	60
Mystery	63
Oak Street Gold	67
Laguna Noir	69
Before Sleep	71
It's On!	77
Sli Dog's Surf Camp	78
Fear and Trembling…and the Best Coffee	83
November Glass	85
Coyotes	86
Plein Air	90
Bougainvillea	95
The Good Gardener	97
Aloe	98
Monterey Formation, as Seen at Crystal Cove Beach	103
Crystal Cove	104
A Book at the Beach	107

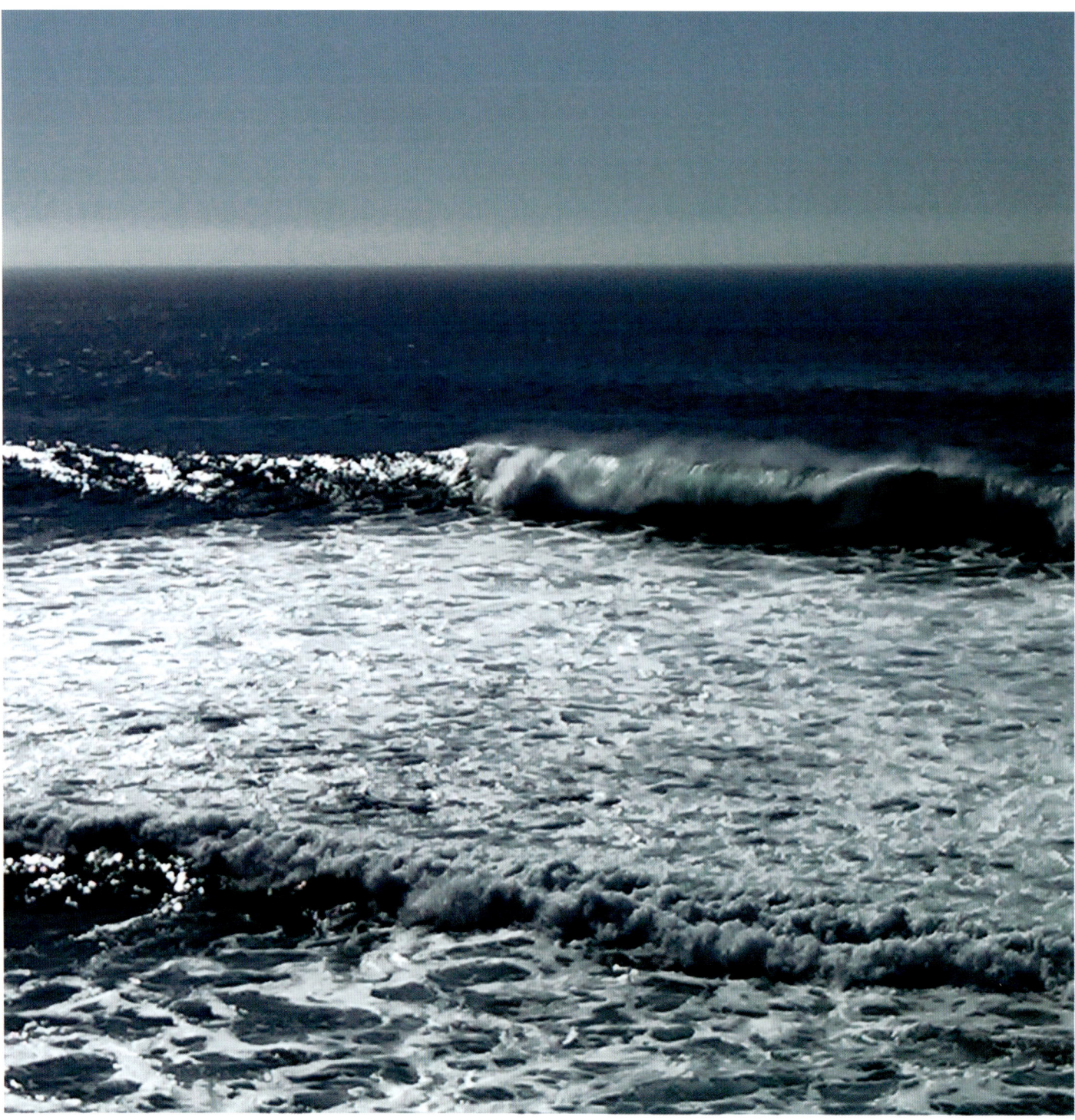

West Swell

Last night I opened
the bedroom windows to better hear
the west swell announcing its arrival.
In the dark, the building surf sounded like
the thunderous steps of an ill-tempered giant.

This morning, the swell
had filled in and taken on
a different sound, a brisk and friendly crashing.
Under a clear blue sky, the mood at Heisler Park was festive:
surfers hastily parked their cars to check the conditions at Rockpile;
runners slowed their steps to look at the break;
a dog-walker stopped and stared
at a surfer tracing lines across a big set wave.
The giant was nowhere in sight.

Catalina Island After the Rain

Catalina shows
her green curves and golden cliffs,
then fades into gray.

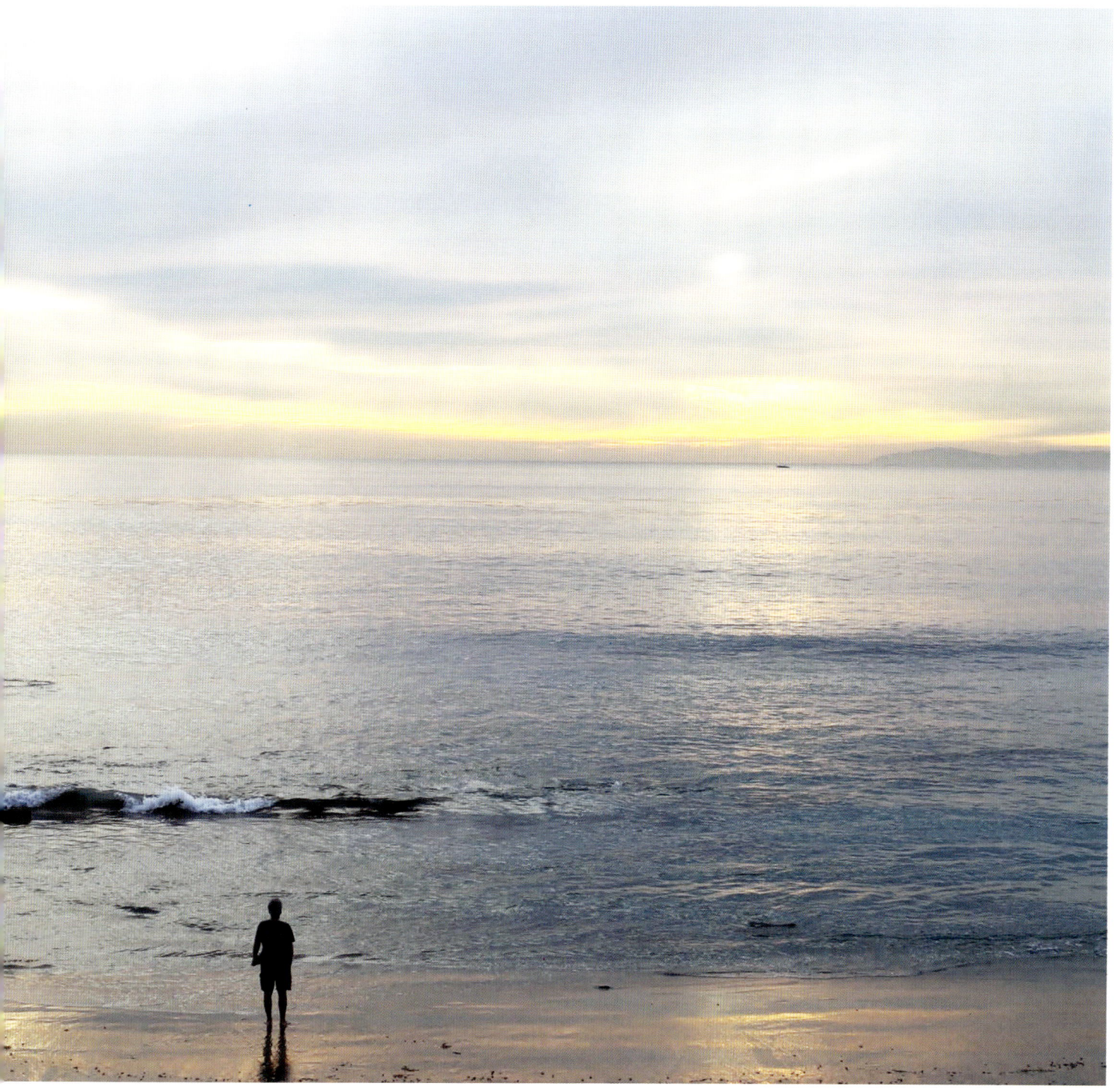

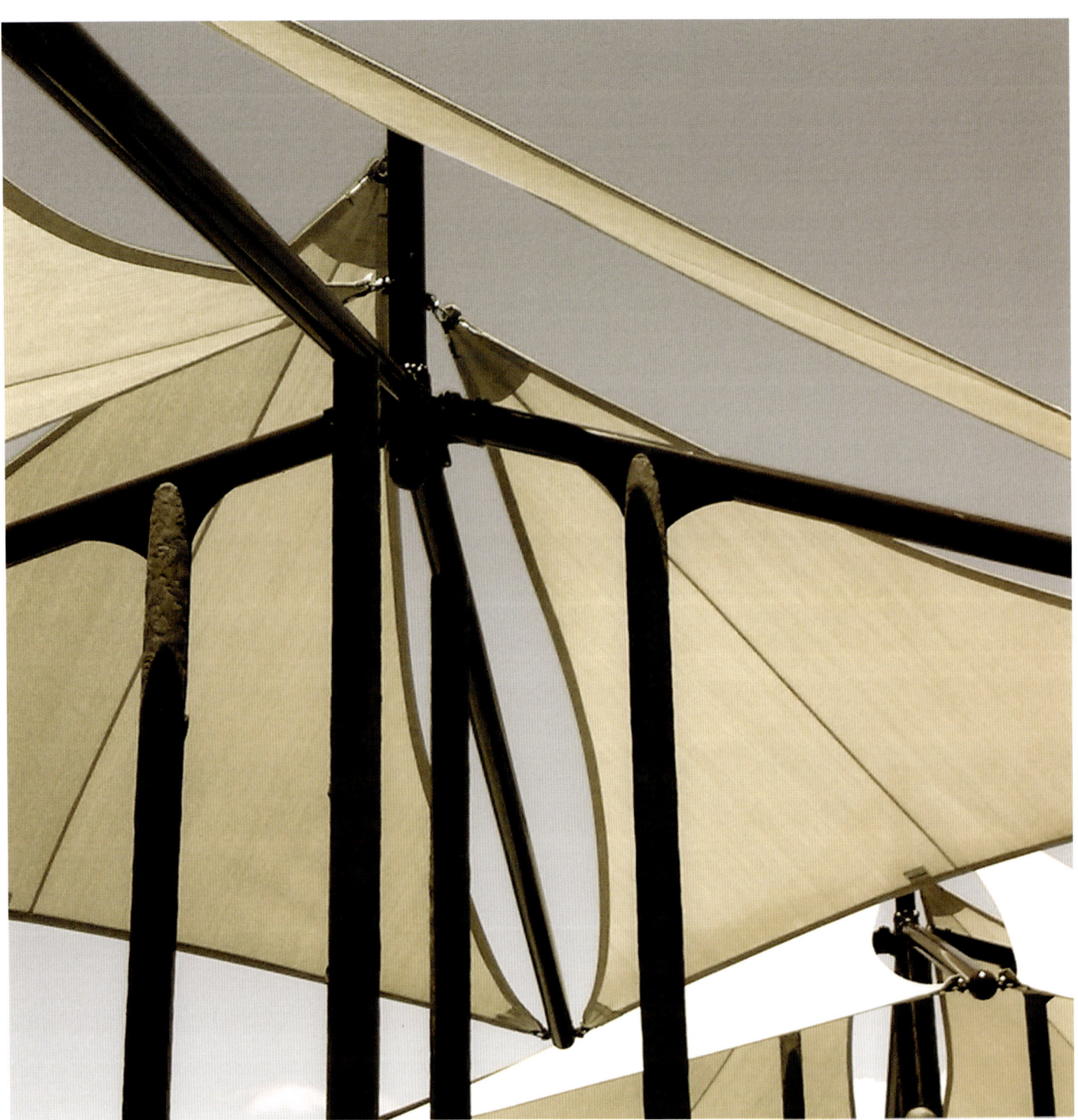

Open and Shut

The day unfurls,
yielding tentative winter sunshine.
Tennis players shed layers as they warm up and start to sweat.
A child's birthday party is set up, a riot of shiny balloons
against a milky sky.
Mountain bikers speed out on the trails
and disappear into sagebrush.

Then, a change:
It looks like rain.

Jackets go back on as the tennis players catch a chill.
A silvery balloon escapes the remains of the birthday party
and drifts away.
The mountain bike riders return in a hurry,
glancing up at the darkening sky.
A cold breeze blows.

It feels like rain;
The day snaps shut.

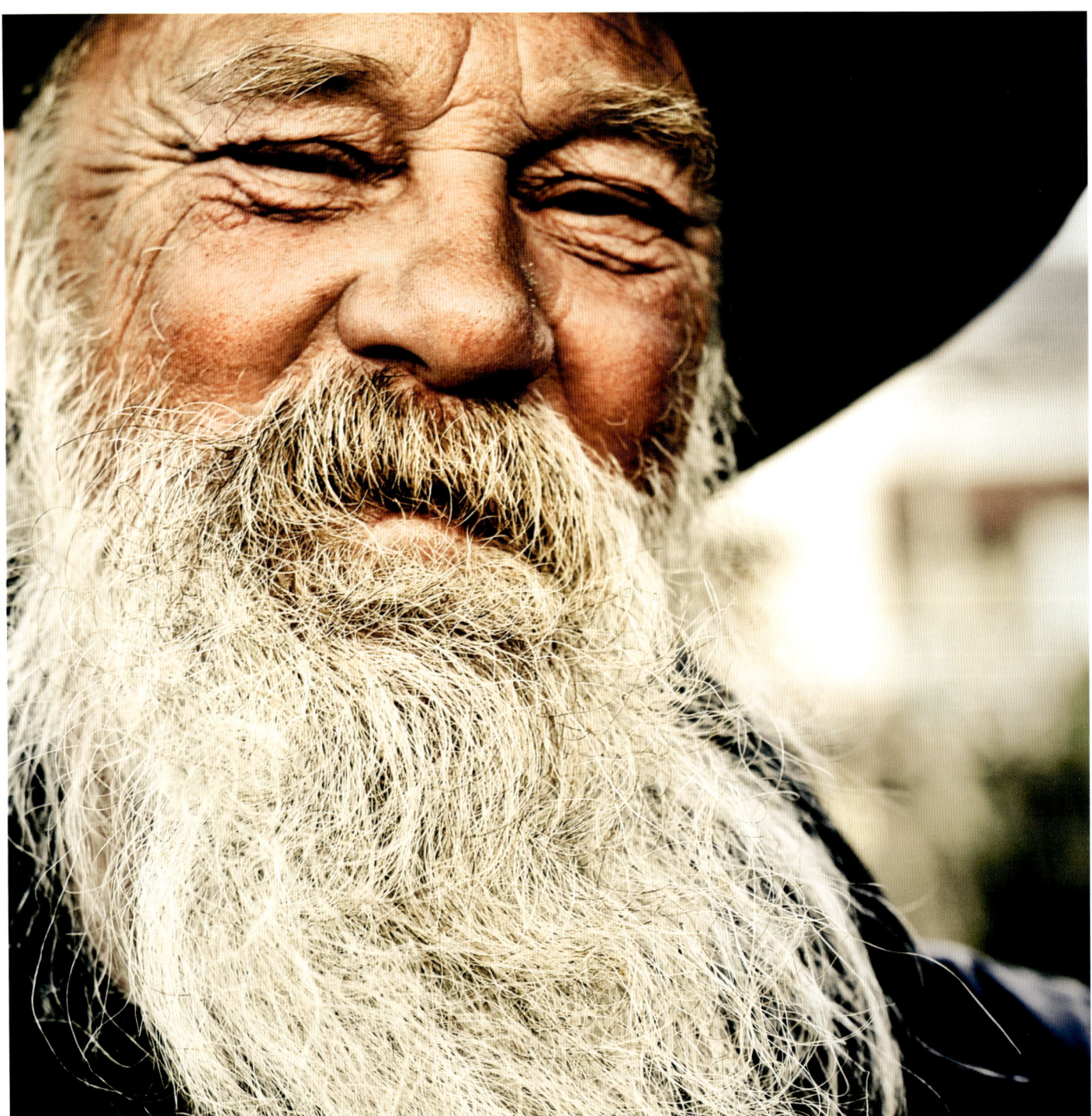

Cowboy, Rest in Peace

"The most recognized of our city's homeless for the past 15 years is dead. 'Cowboy,' Charles Reginald Conwell, 58, was struck and killed in the 1700 block of Laguna Canyon Road at 6:34 Saturday evening."

The icon of Heisler Park,
the skinny, jangly, boot-wearing standard-bearer
of the way things used to be:
Cowboy, rest in peace.

Cowboy and his kind, "hobos,"
my children call them romantically,
were model vagrants then, their only crime:
public intoxication
again and again and again.

Summer's sad, urgent wave of squatters—
younger, more violent—made him a relic.
Memories of Frisbee games on the boardwalk
with Cowboy had to be set aside.
It was serious now.
Time was short, people afraid.

Did Cowboy sense that his kind was obsolete?
That the days of hobos jumping trains,
of benign town drunks receiving the blessing of the locals,
were no more?
Did he feel a push—
changing times, fallen economies, shifting populations
—and surrender?

Cowboy, rest in peace.

"Police said he was hit by a mini-van heading west on Laguna Canyon Road as he walked across and into the path of the van. He was not in a crosswalk, police said. It was unknown if he was en route to the homeless sleeping facility located close by.

Conwell was knocked off the roadway and the police log indicated that he was '...bleeding, breathing and unconscious....' Paramedics took him to Mission Hospital Laguna Beach where he was pronounced dead a short time after his arrival."

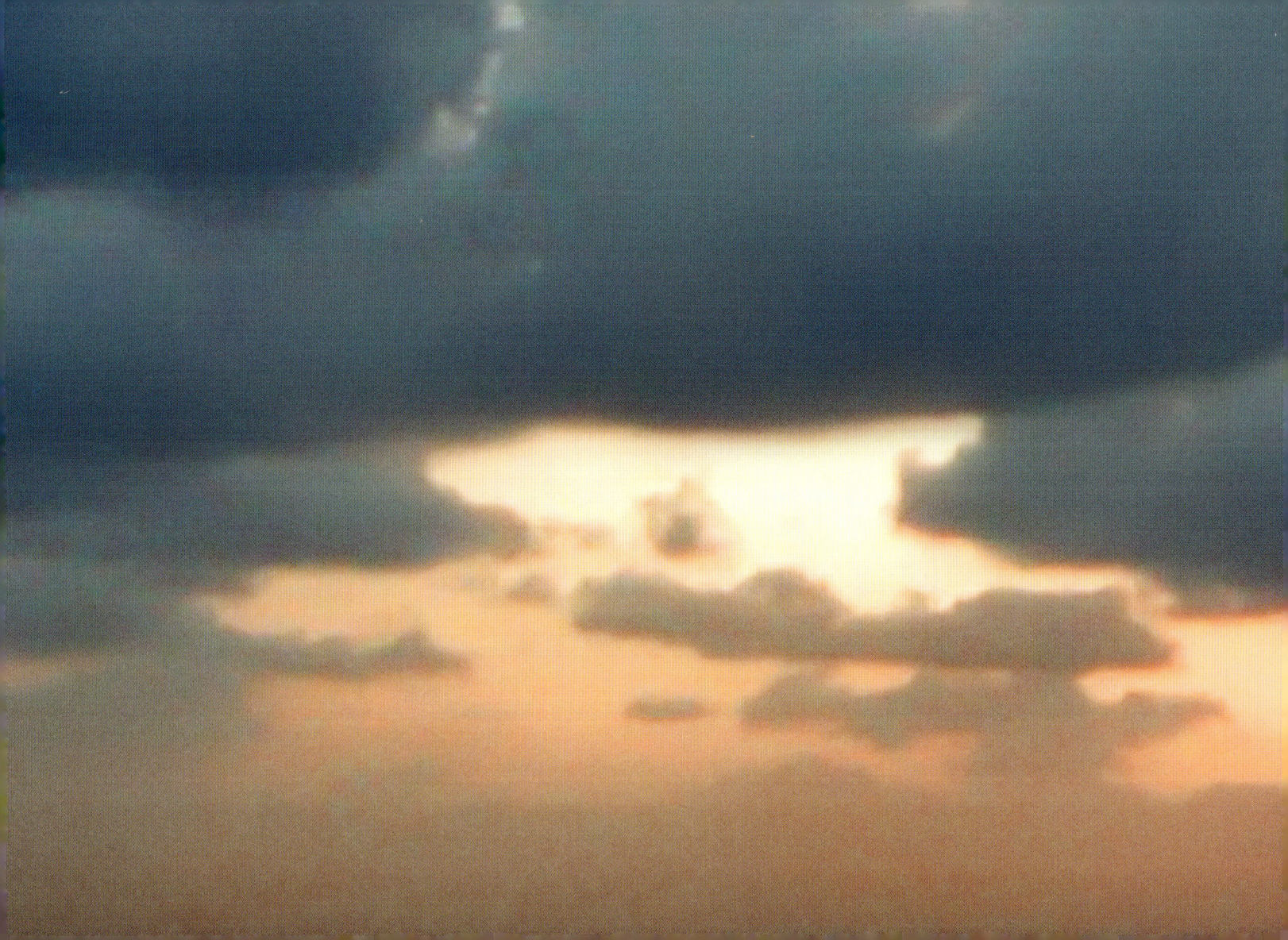

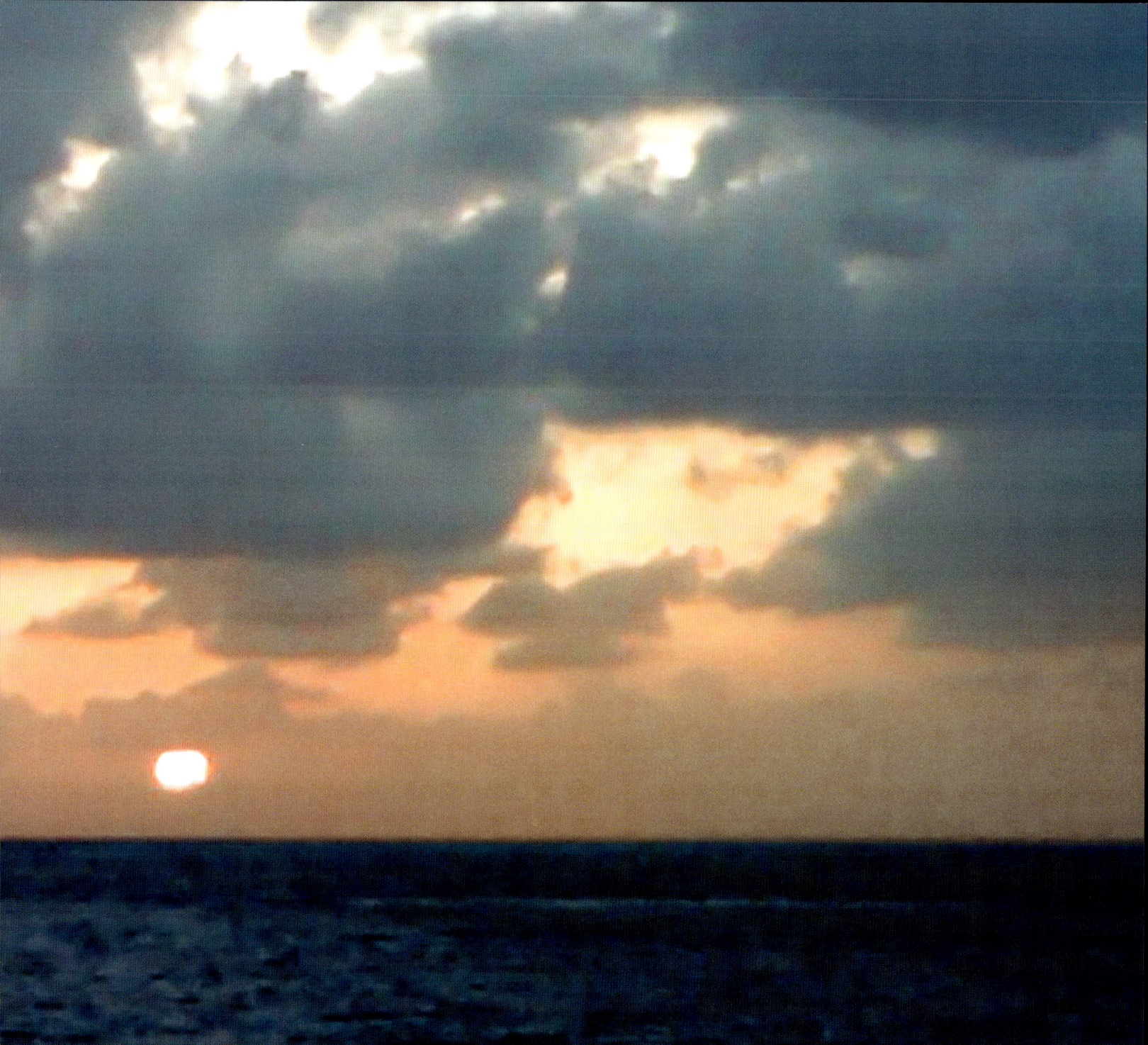

Heart and Torch:
In Memory of Rick Griffin,
an Honorary Lagunan
if Ever There Was one

Your drawings of
breaking waves,
flying eyeballs,
swirling colors
and sacred hearts
tell me that even when you were here,
you weren't really here.
You were never of this world
and left it a little early.
I look at your eyes
in a black and white photograph,
your hair and beard as wild as John the Baptist's
might have been,
and wish you could tell me
what you're seeing now.

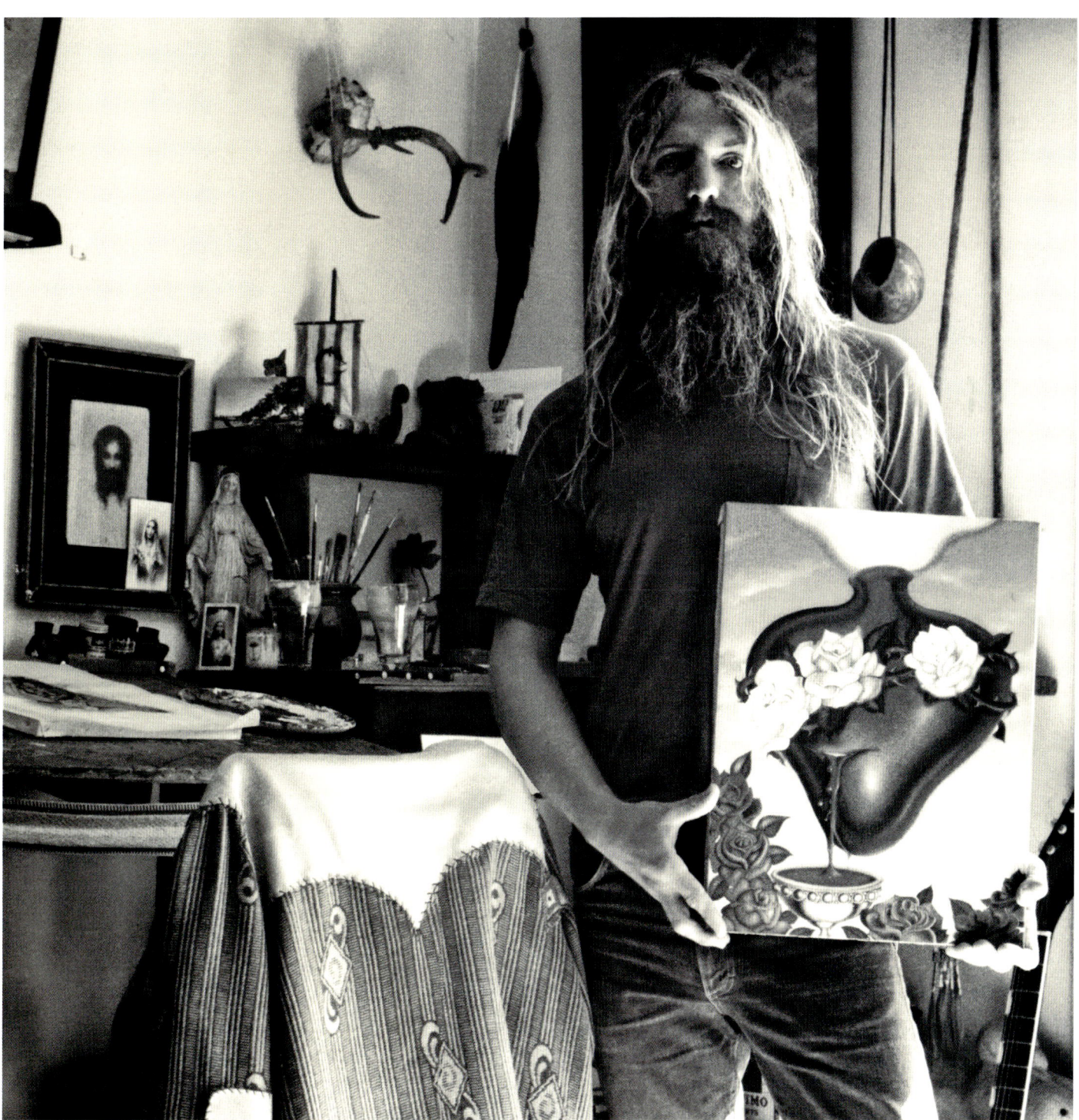

Friday Night Lights

Houses on the hill
light up one by one; a pale
moon shines through the clouds.

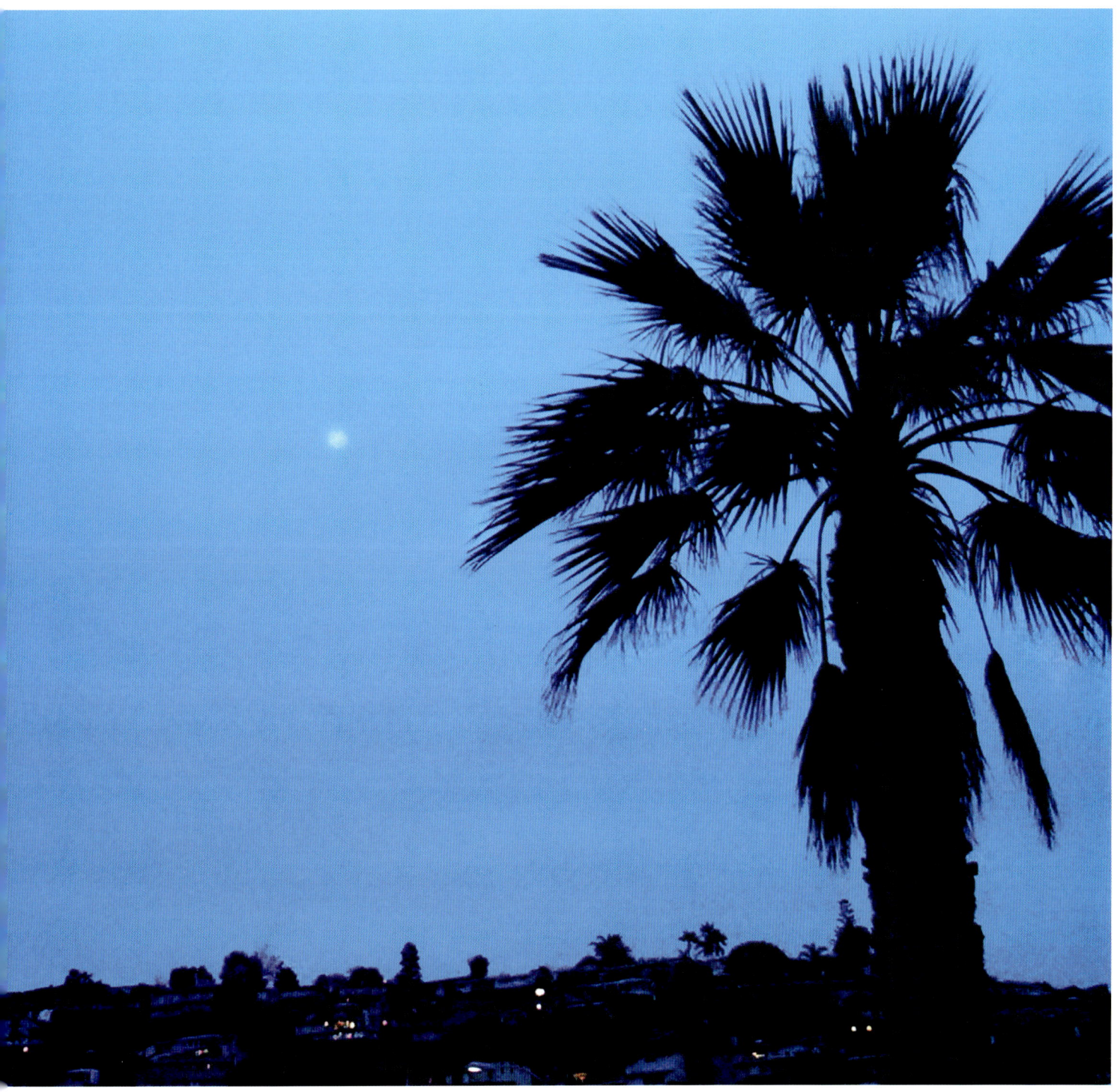

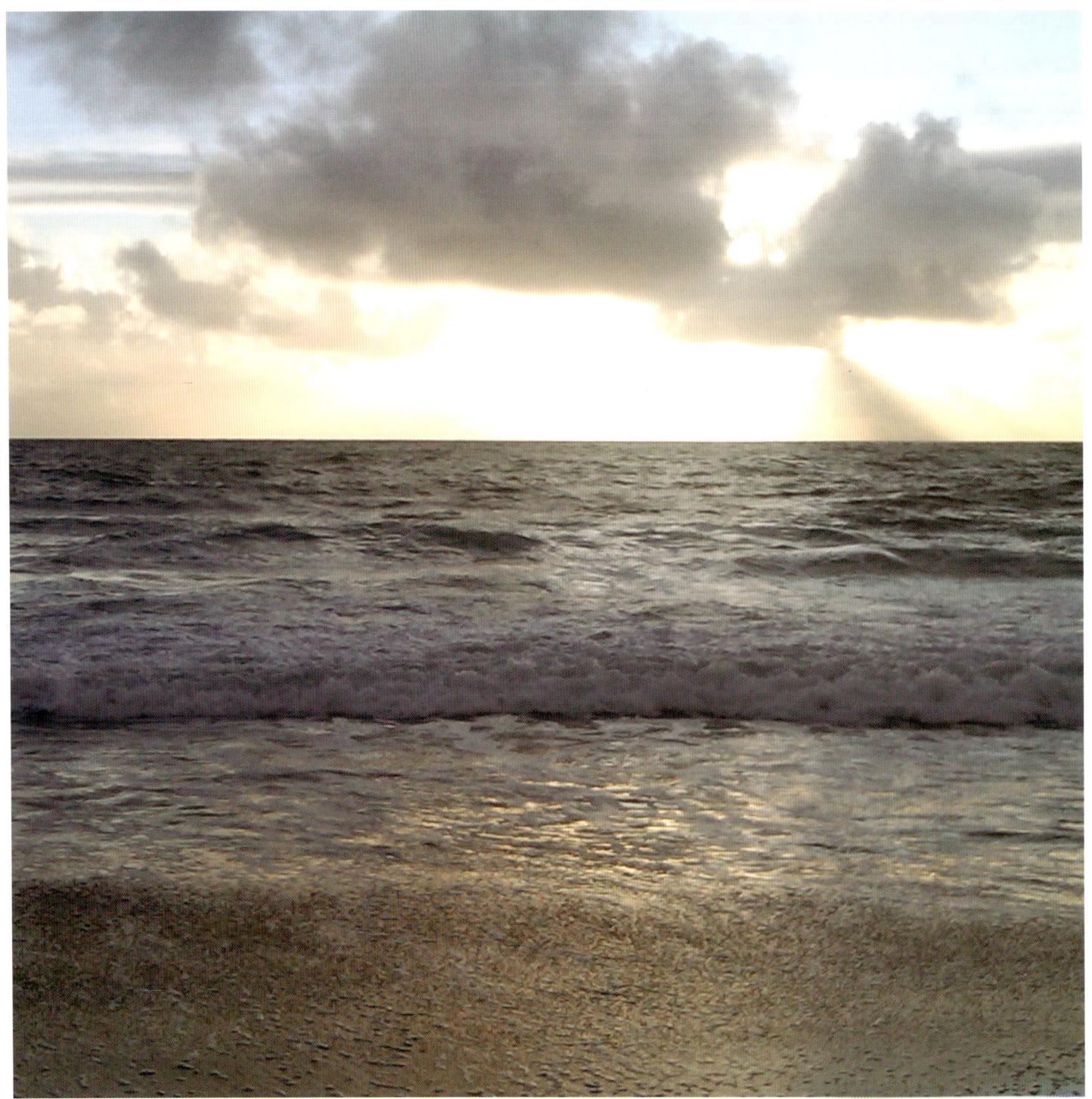

Brooks Street After the Rain

iridescent sand
clouds of gold and silver, air
so clean it shimmers

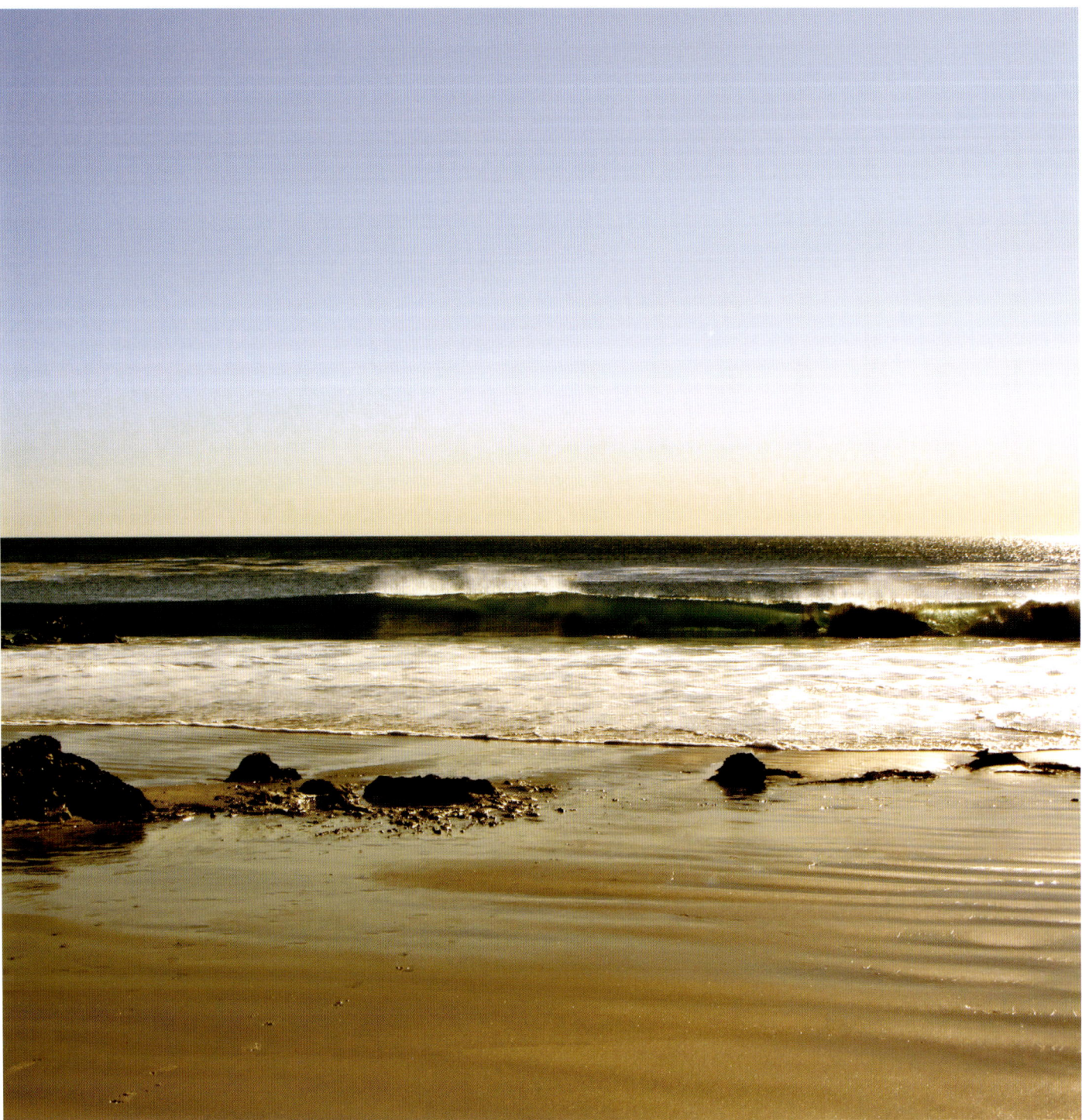

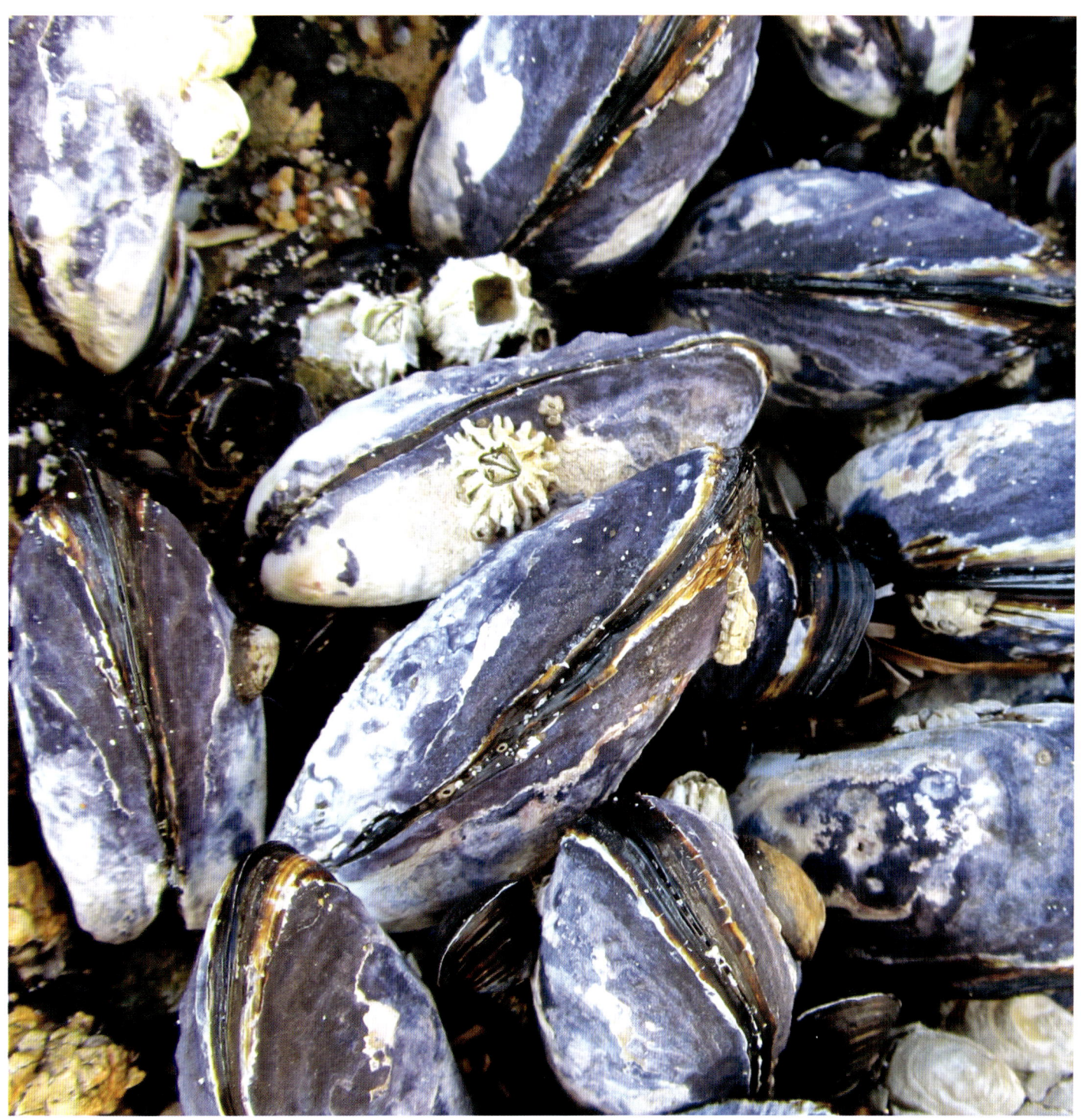

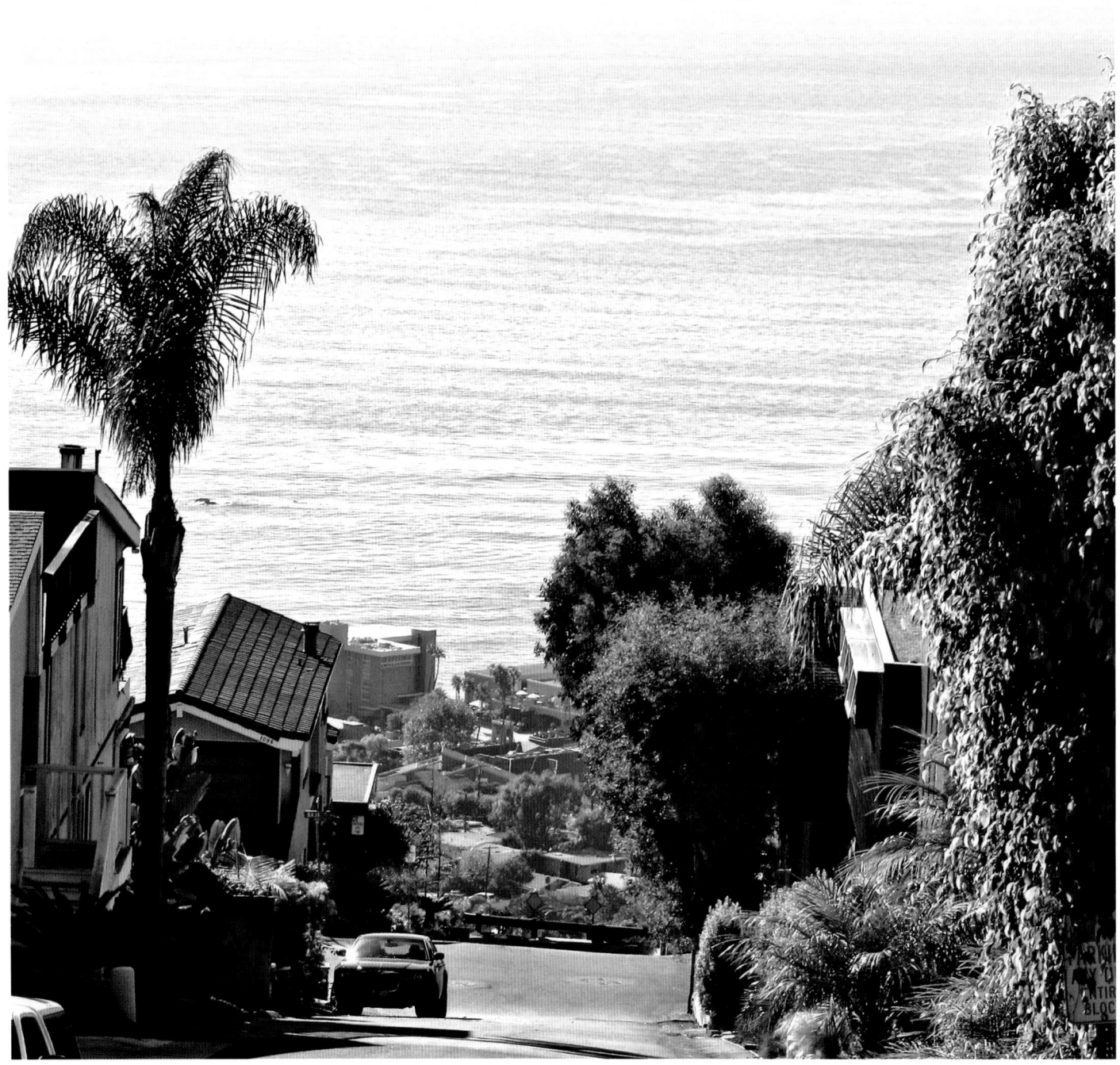

Del Mar Avenue

the road is so steep
      and the ocean so blue I
            may stop and dive in

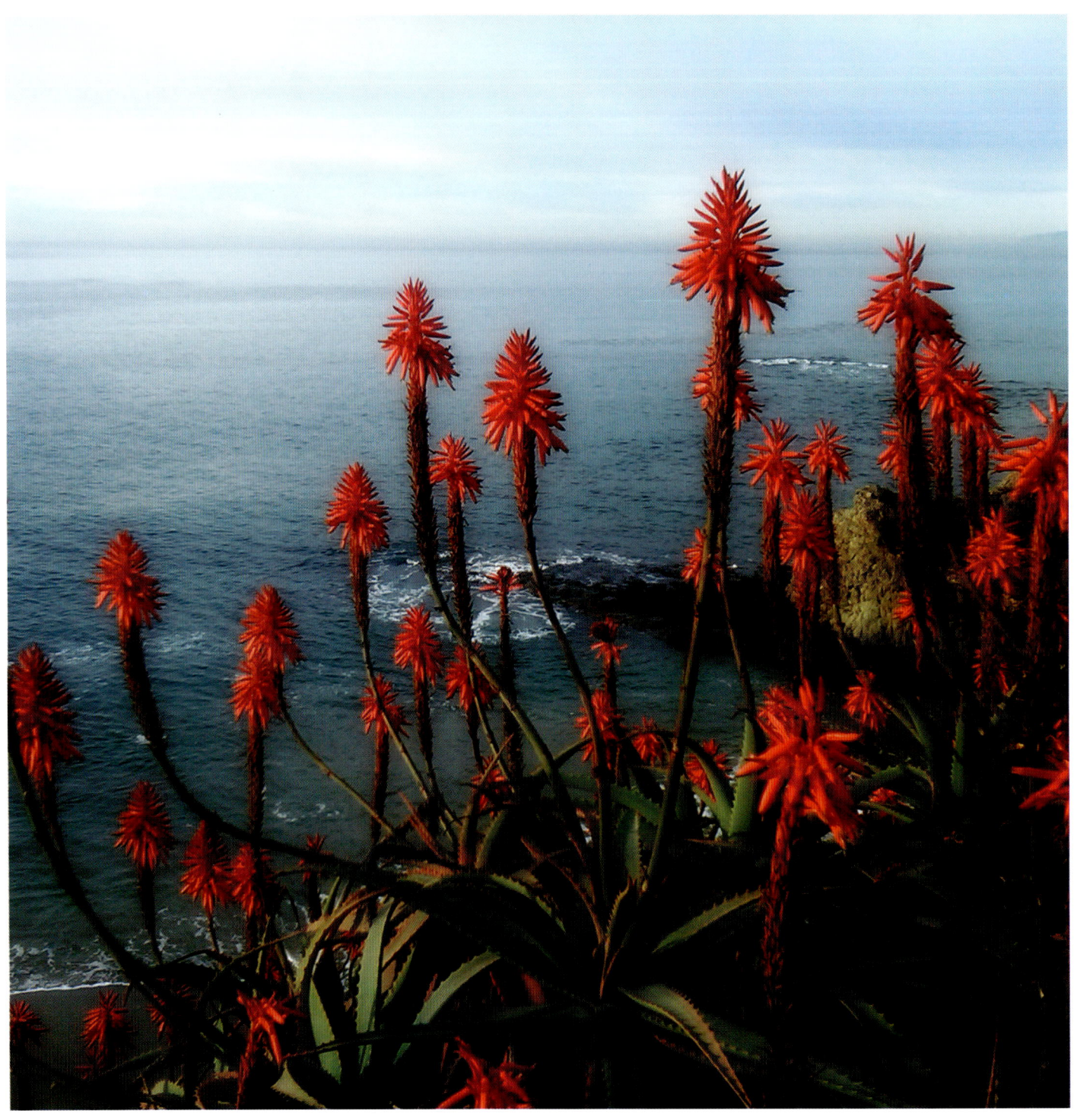

Heisler Park in Winter

Aloe is in bloom,
spilling orange-red flowers
down the hill toward the
ocean. A surfer, riding
the remains of a
fading swell, skims across the
face of a wave at
Rockpile. A gray-haired woman,
backpack at her feet,
sits on a bench, her face turned
up to the soft winter sun.

All Things New

As I walked along the shore
the old order of things passed away.
The cars, parking lots
shops and stoplights
disappeared behind bluffs;
layers of millennia
drowned out the sound of traffic.
It was quiet then
but for the rushing, breaking waves
and—
barely audible—
silvery voices calling
Alpha and Omega
First and Last
Beginning and End

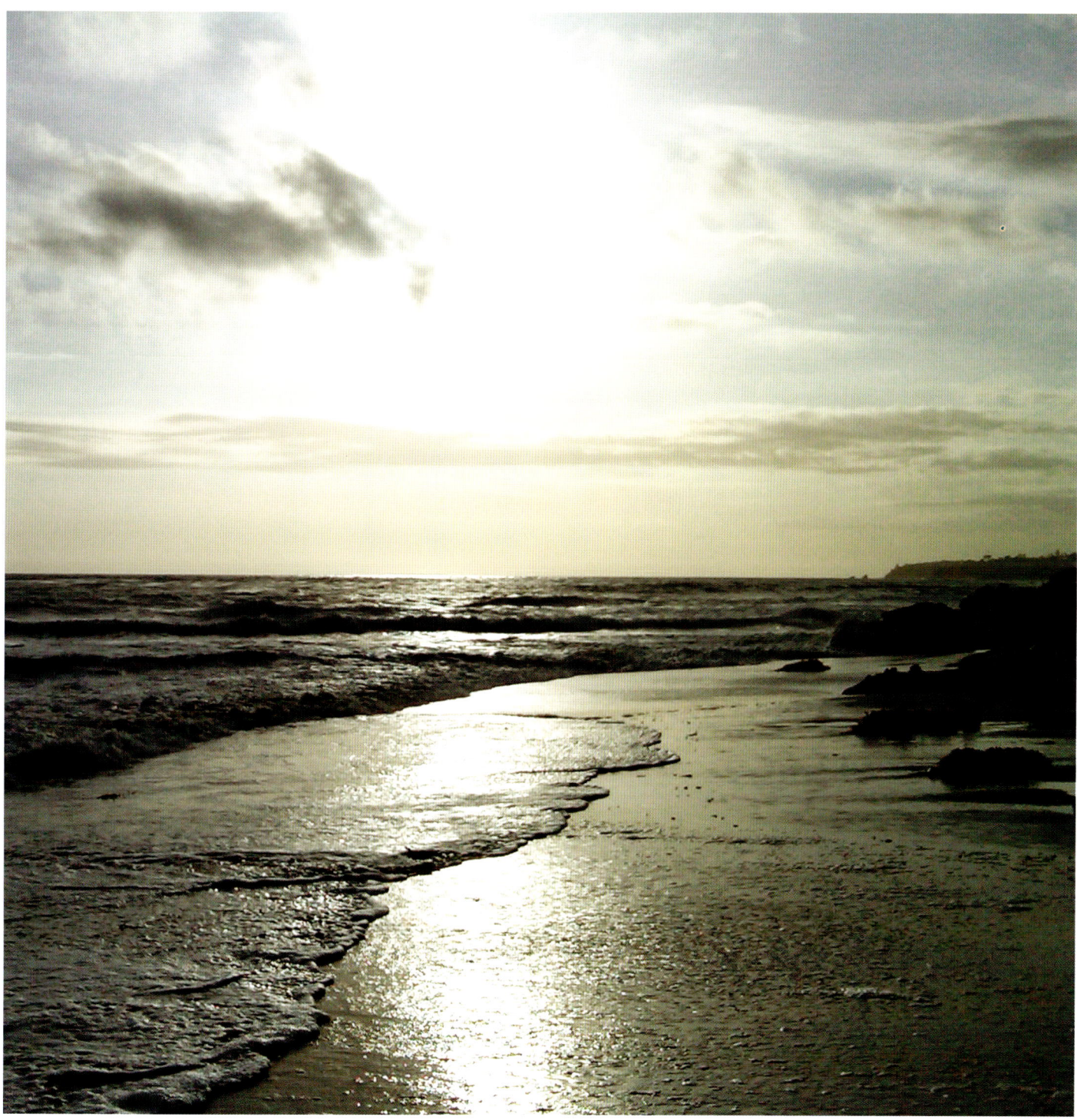

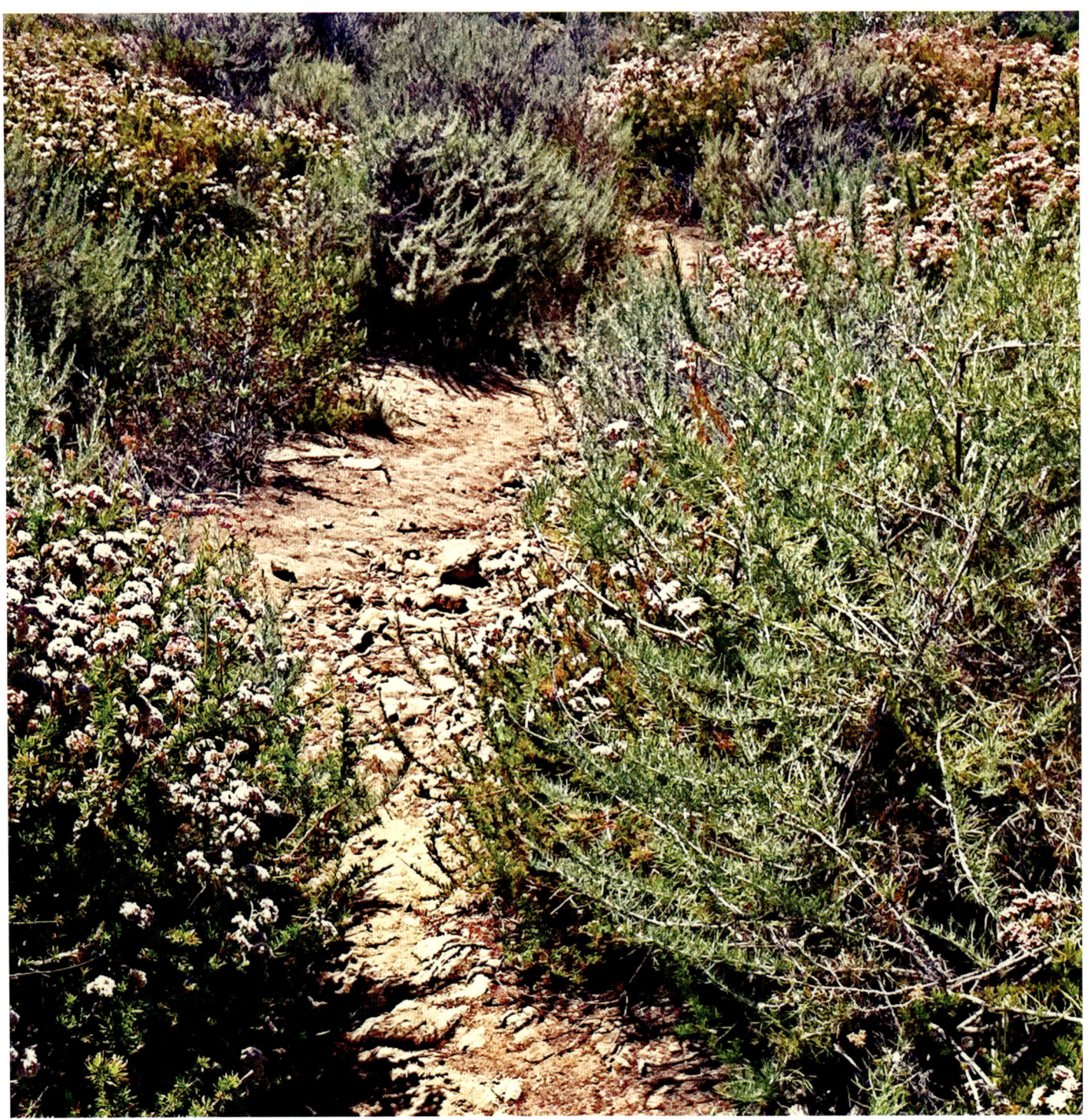

Hike

Two women hiked toward me
on the trail, water bottles in hand.
As they approached
and then passed me,
the older one in the hat
was saying forcefully
in a clear voice
Well I've read that book and I've studied
what all the other religious traditions say
about personal growth
and what I've found—
at which point I turned my head
hoping to hear what she had found
but then we were too far apart
and her voice was lost on the wind.

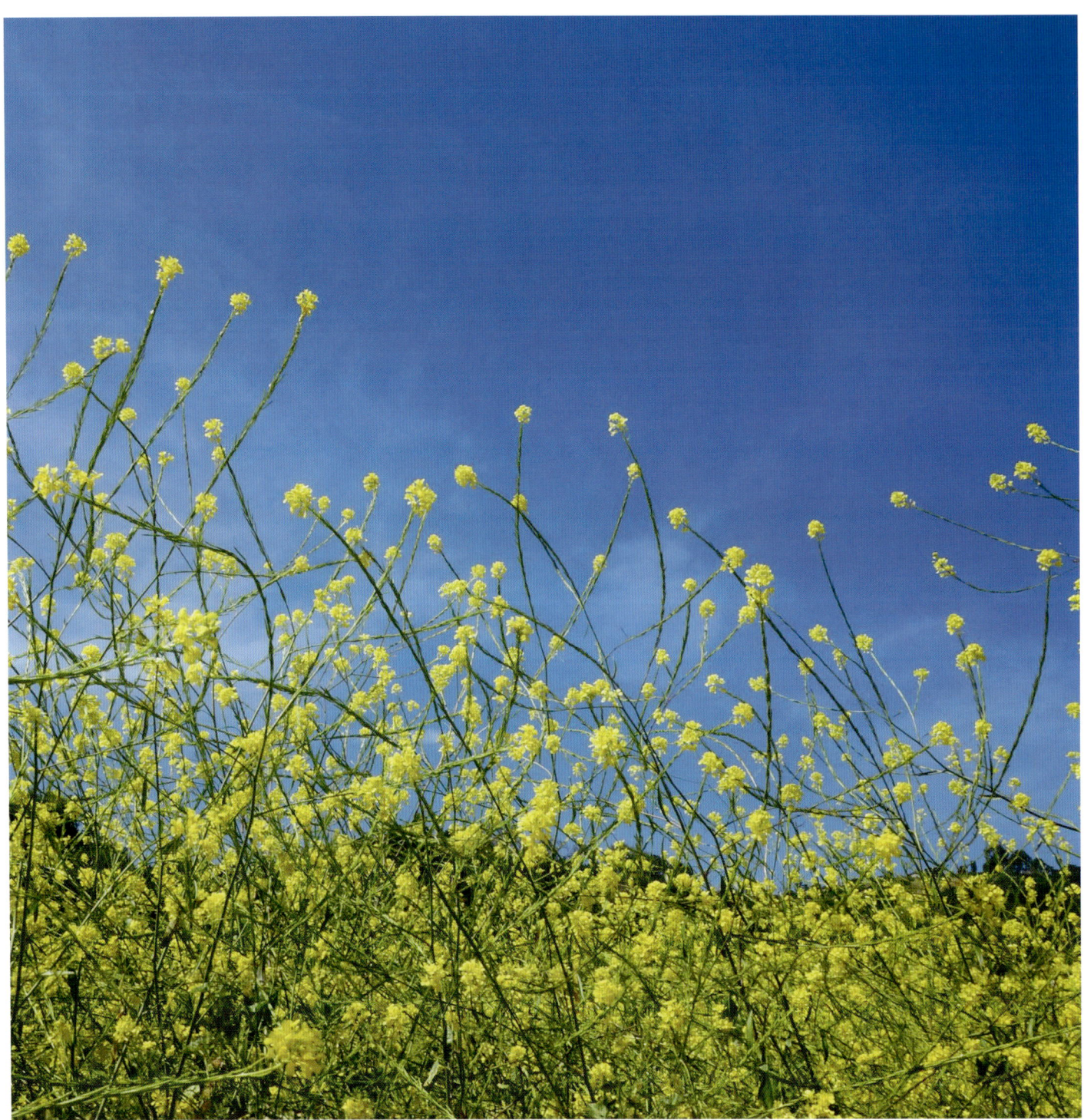

Mustard

A Saturday hike
like any other…but wait!
The mustard's in bloom.

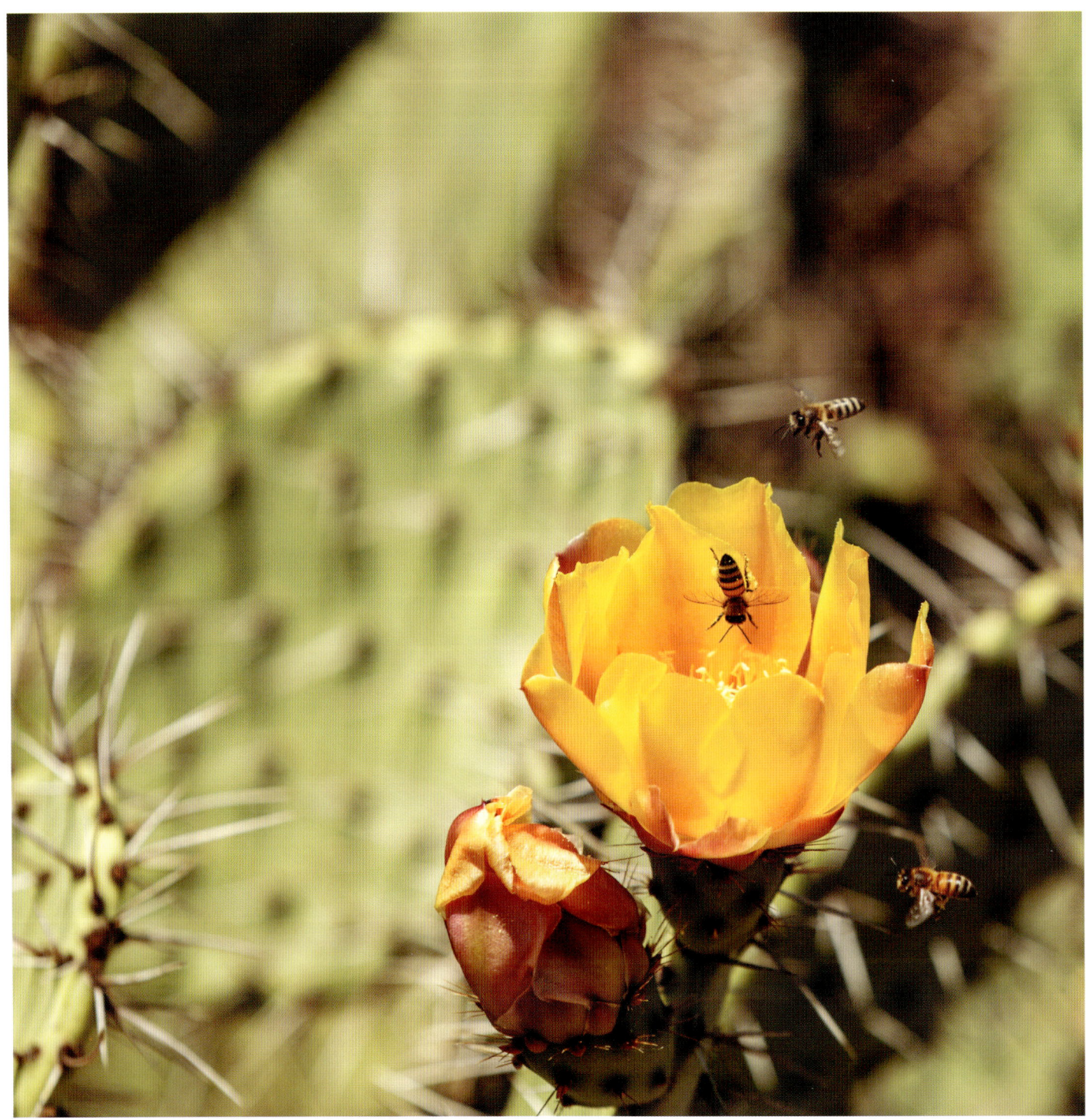

Canyon

Powdery gold underfoot,
muffling my footsteps.
Rustling in the brush. Rabbit?
Rattlesnake? Cacti,
sagebrush. The whir of insect
wings, the wind, mountain
bike gears. Then silence. A hawk
banks, circles above.
Behind me, the hills give way
to the sky and sea.

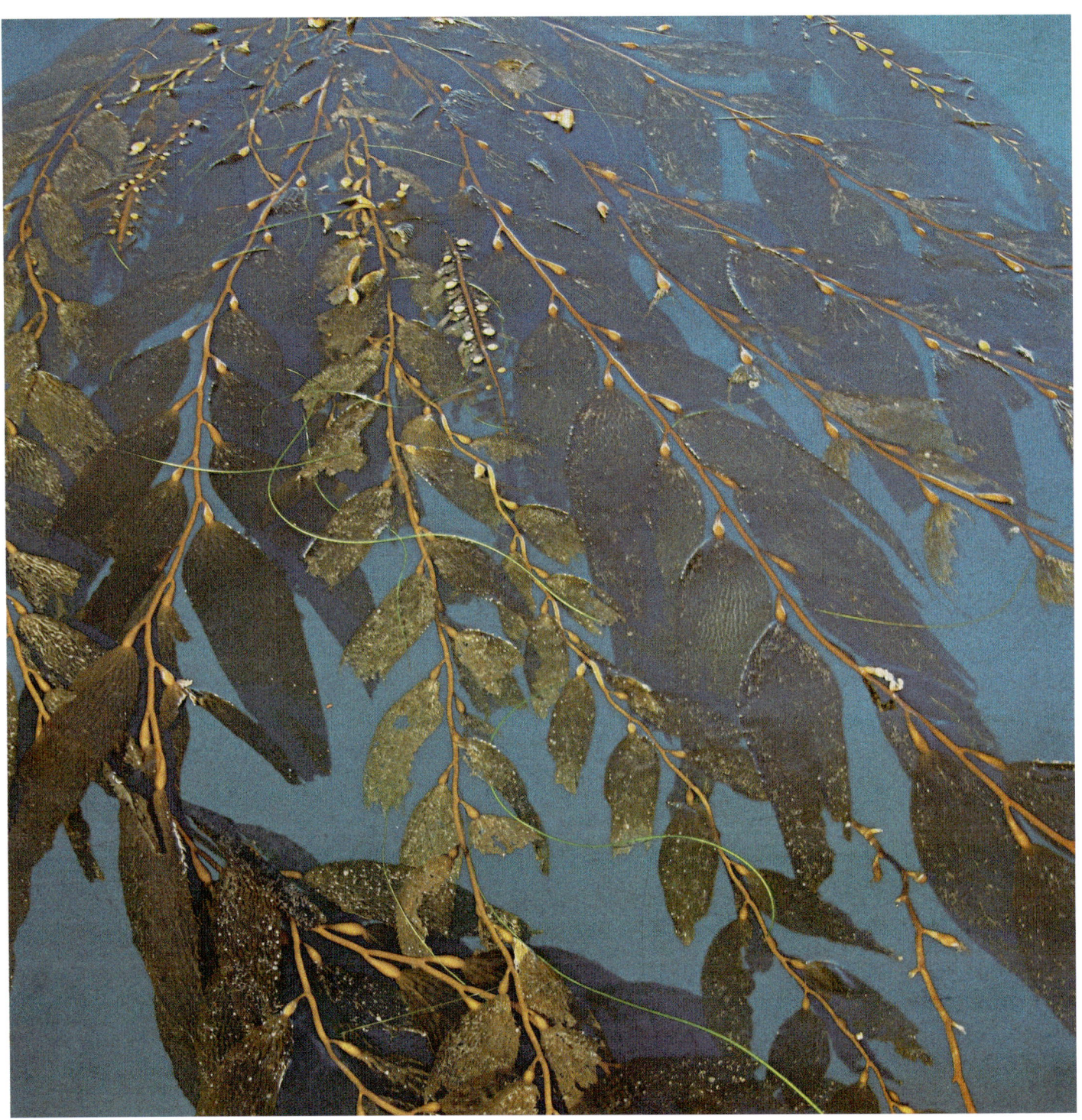

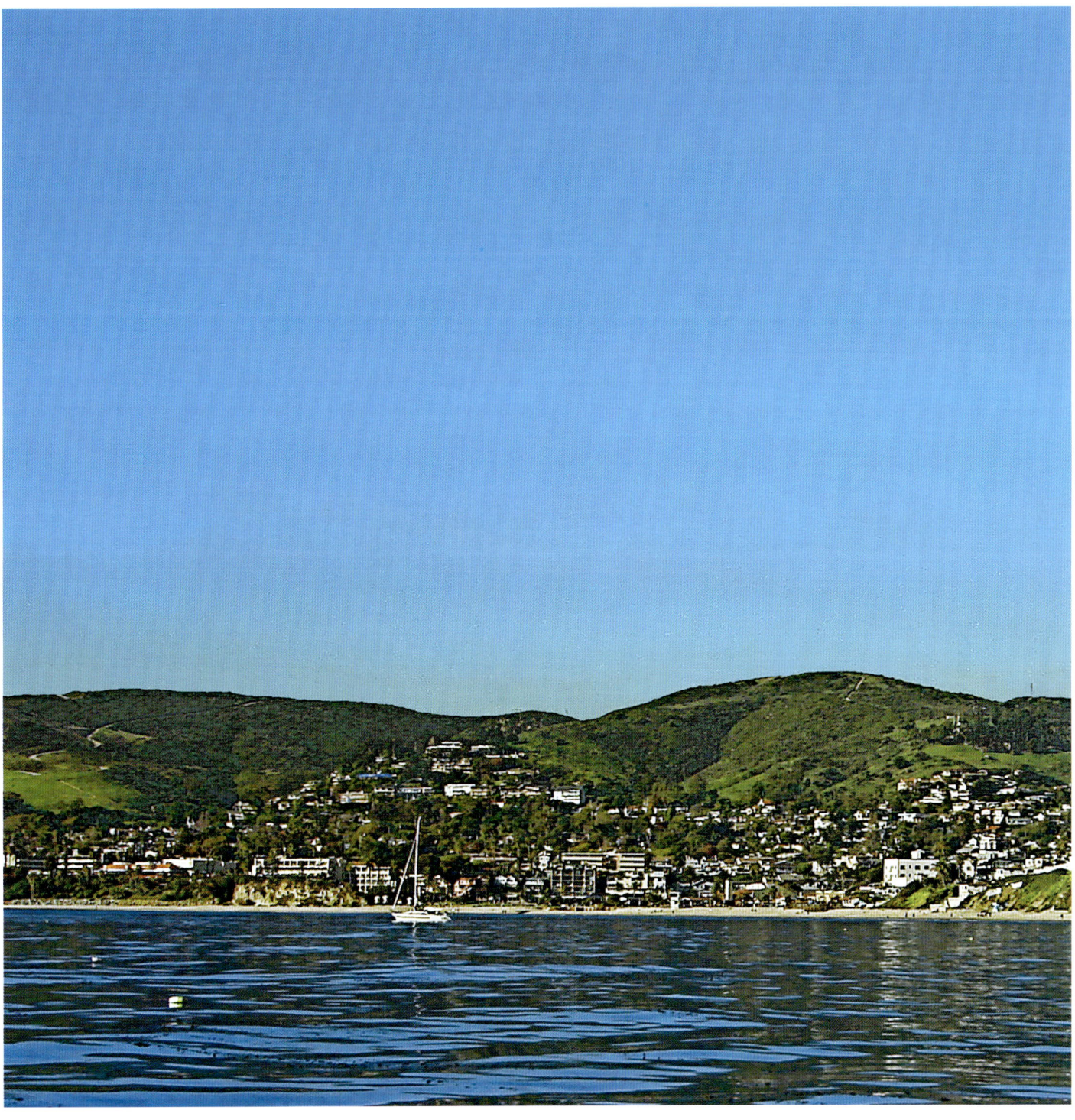

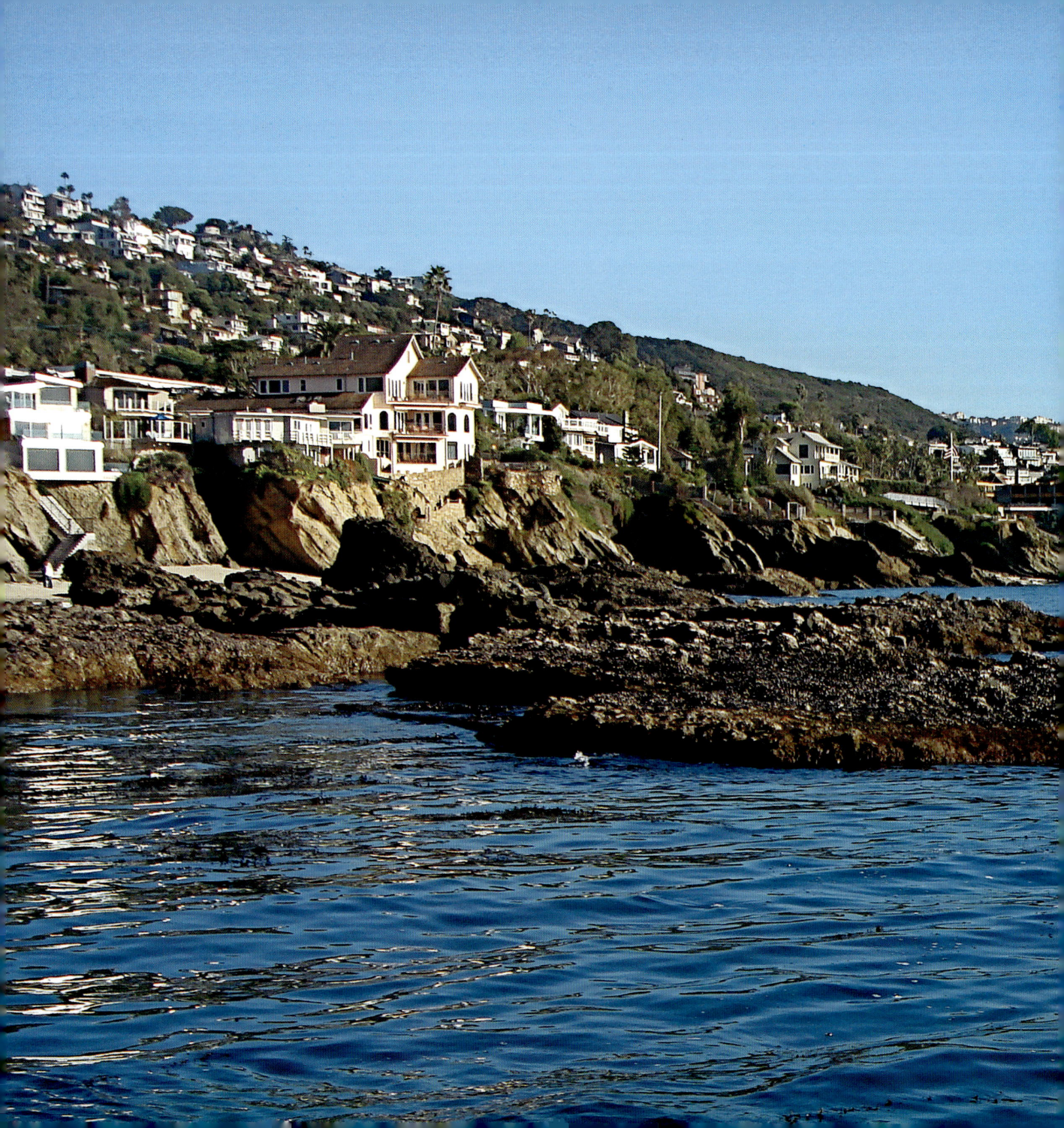

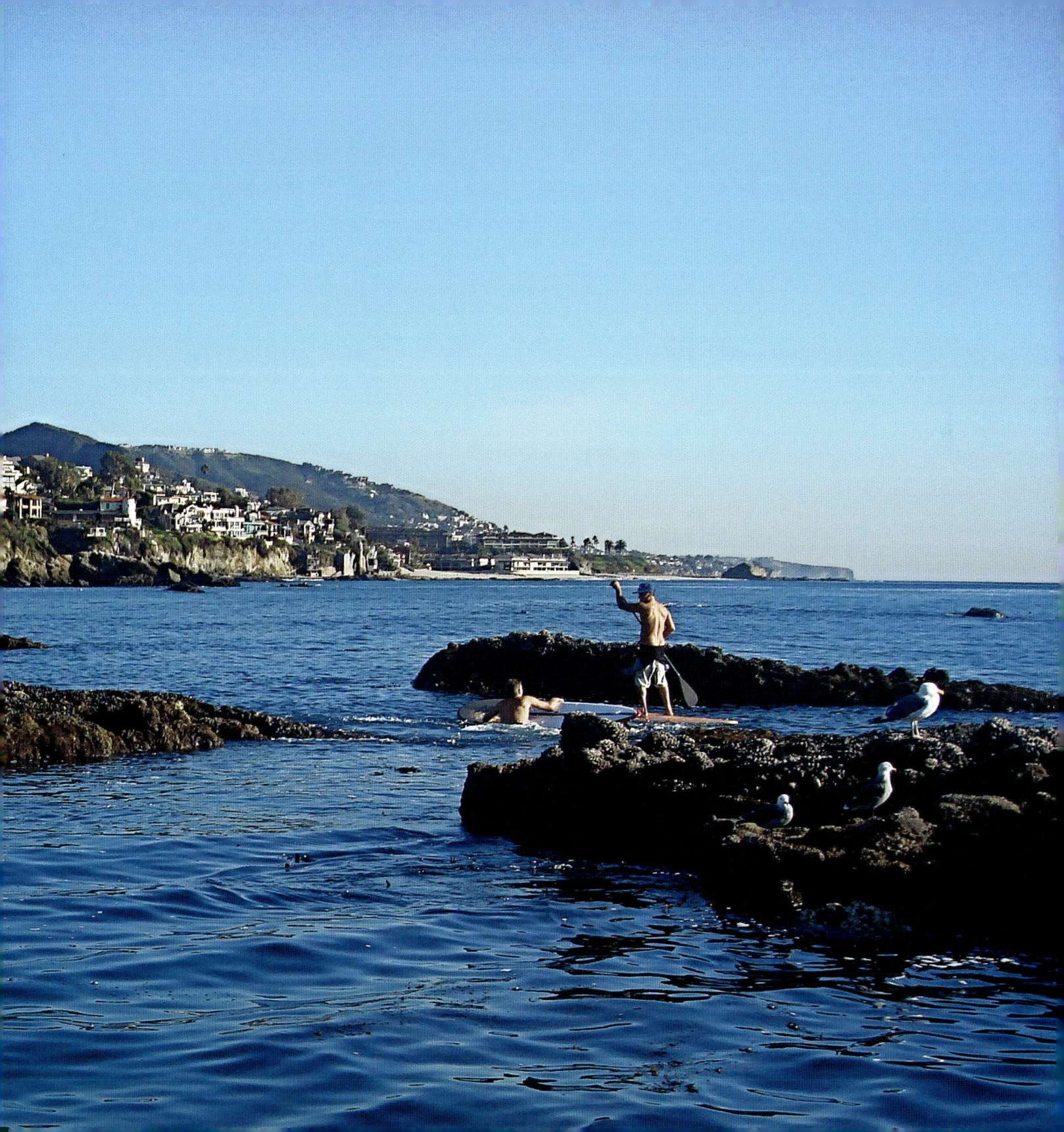

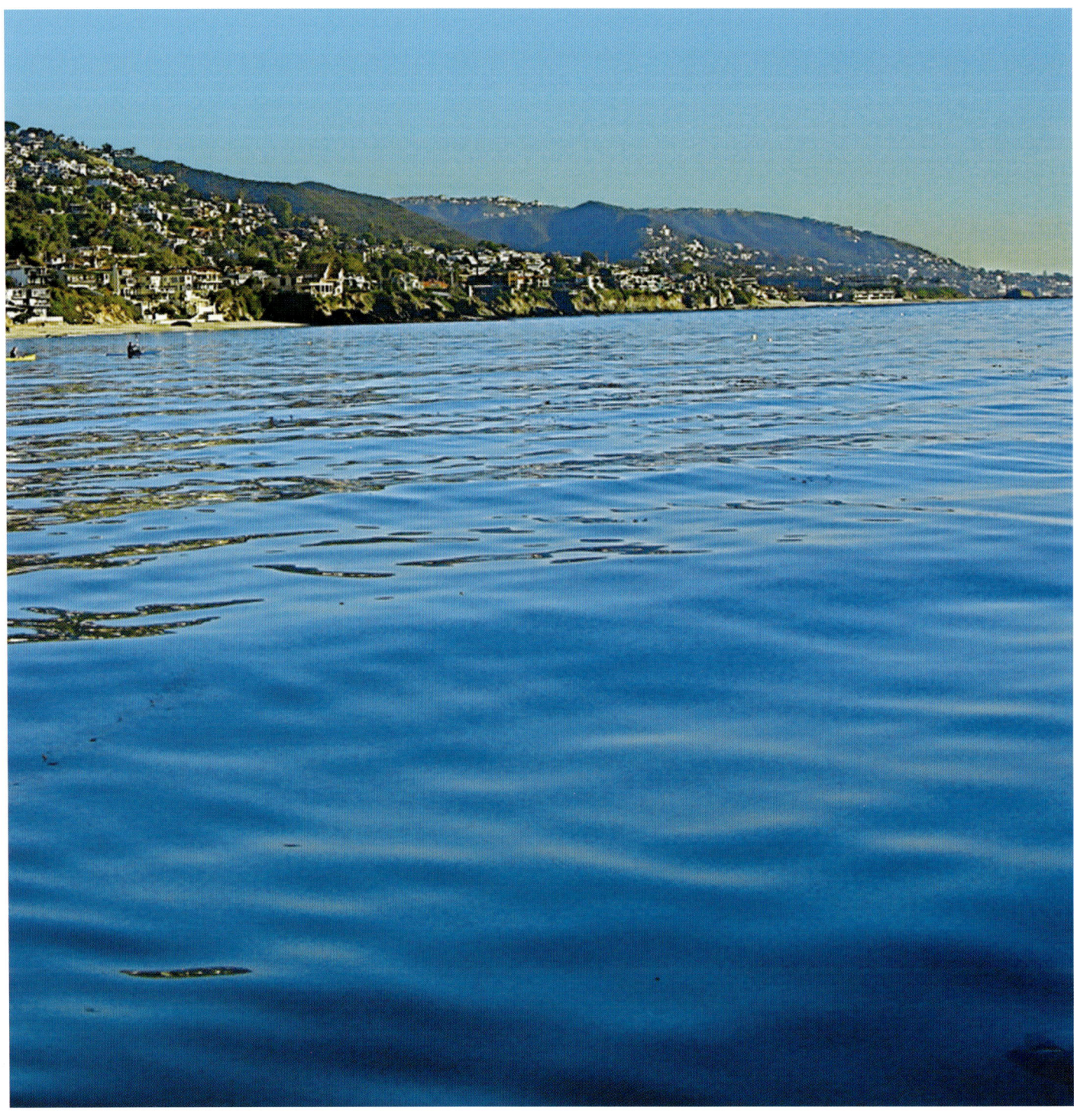

Sea

A mottled black seal
resting in the depths. Drifting,
tethered kelp, teeming
with flashes of silver, flares
of orange. Bird Rock.
A pelican, wings grazing
the water. A lone,
faded sailboat. Waves breaking
on the shore. Farther away,
hills notched by a gold canyon.

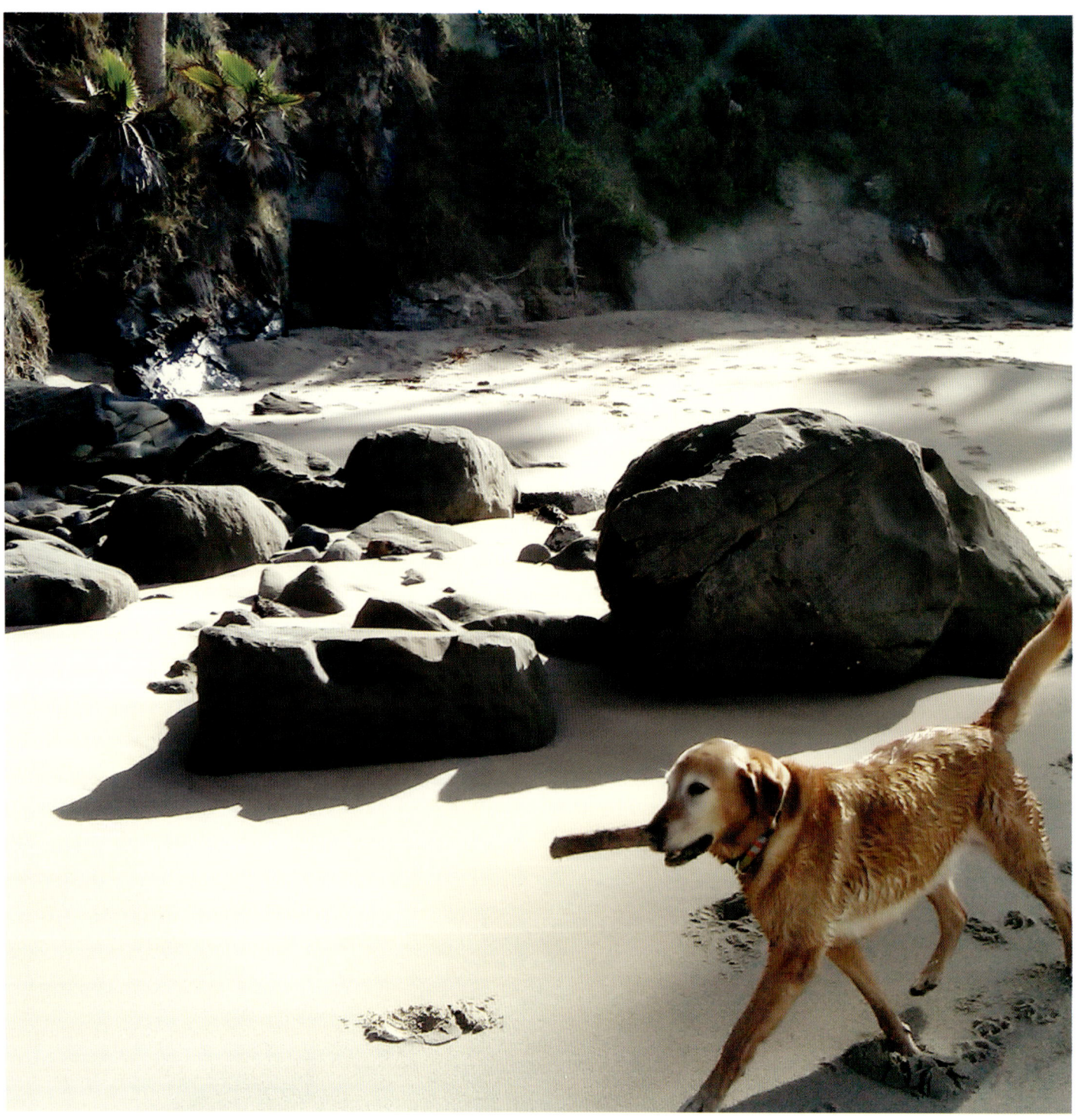

A Good Morning

Coffee at the French
with talk of tides, surf conditions
and that Rothko painting
that seems to breathe.
The dog's morning swim.
Now, let the day begin.

Spring Break

It's only nine in
the morning but Main Beach is
already dotted
with umbrellas and blankets.
A sandcastle is
in the making. Mothers smear
sunscreen on the backs
of their pale, happy children
in Easter-egg hued
swimsuits. Two college kids—
a girl and a boy
in jeans and sweatshirts—sit on
the steps to the boardwalk, still
nursing cans of Coors Light
and blinking in the bright sun.

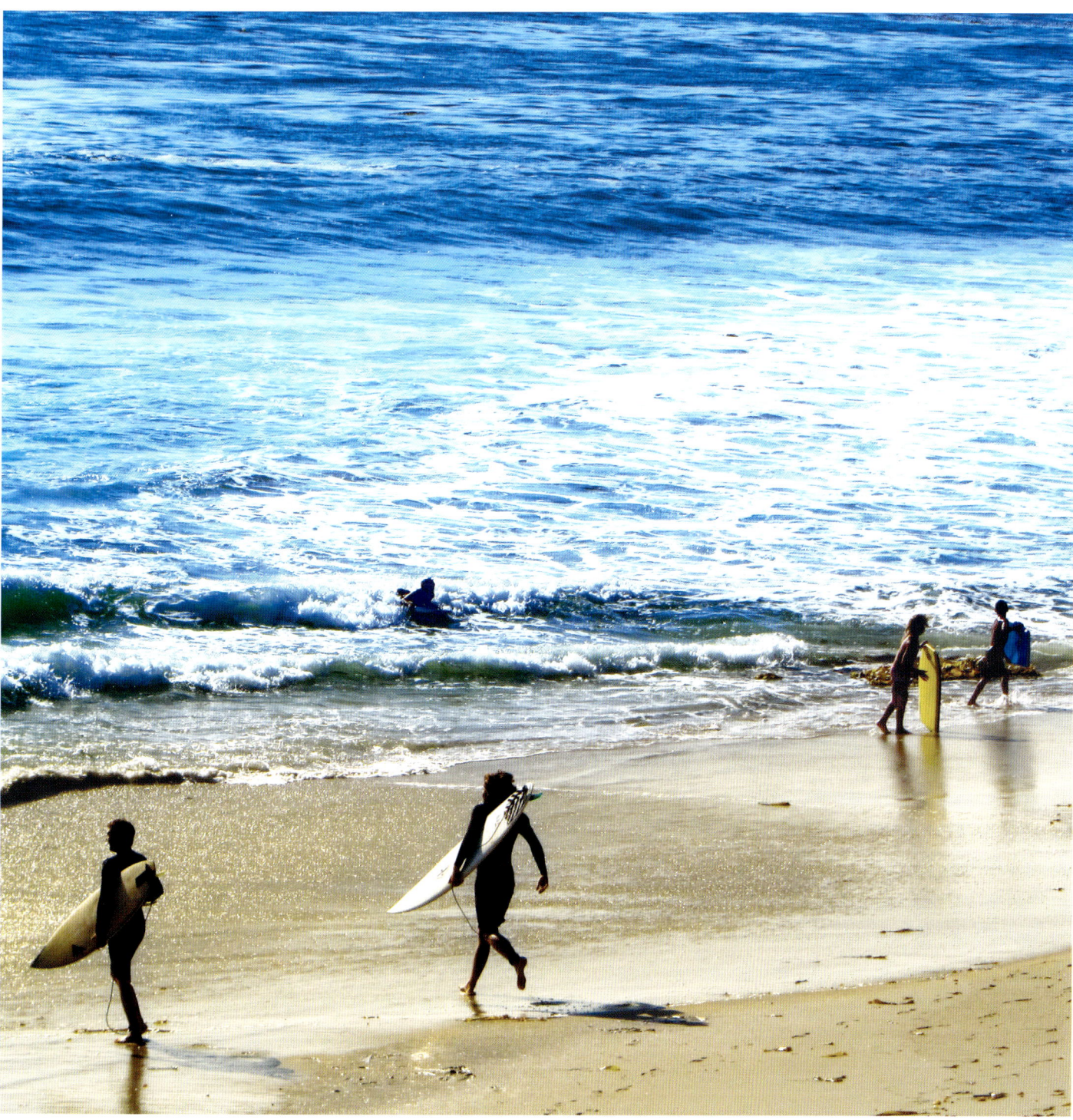

Hakama Glory Day

Cold, green-glass water.
Little waves, the sun on my
face and—ah! Dolphins.

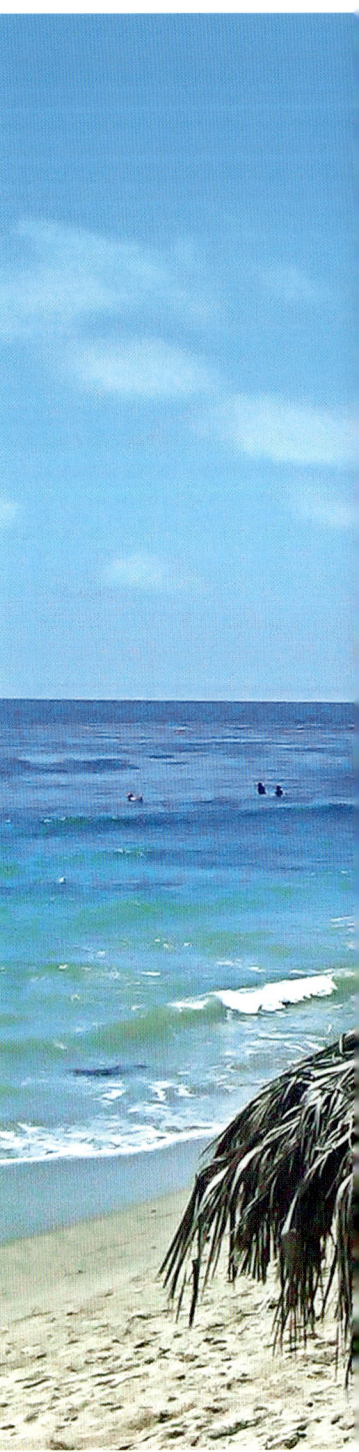

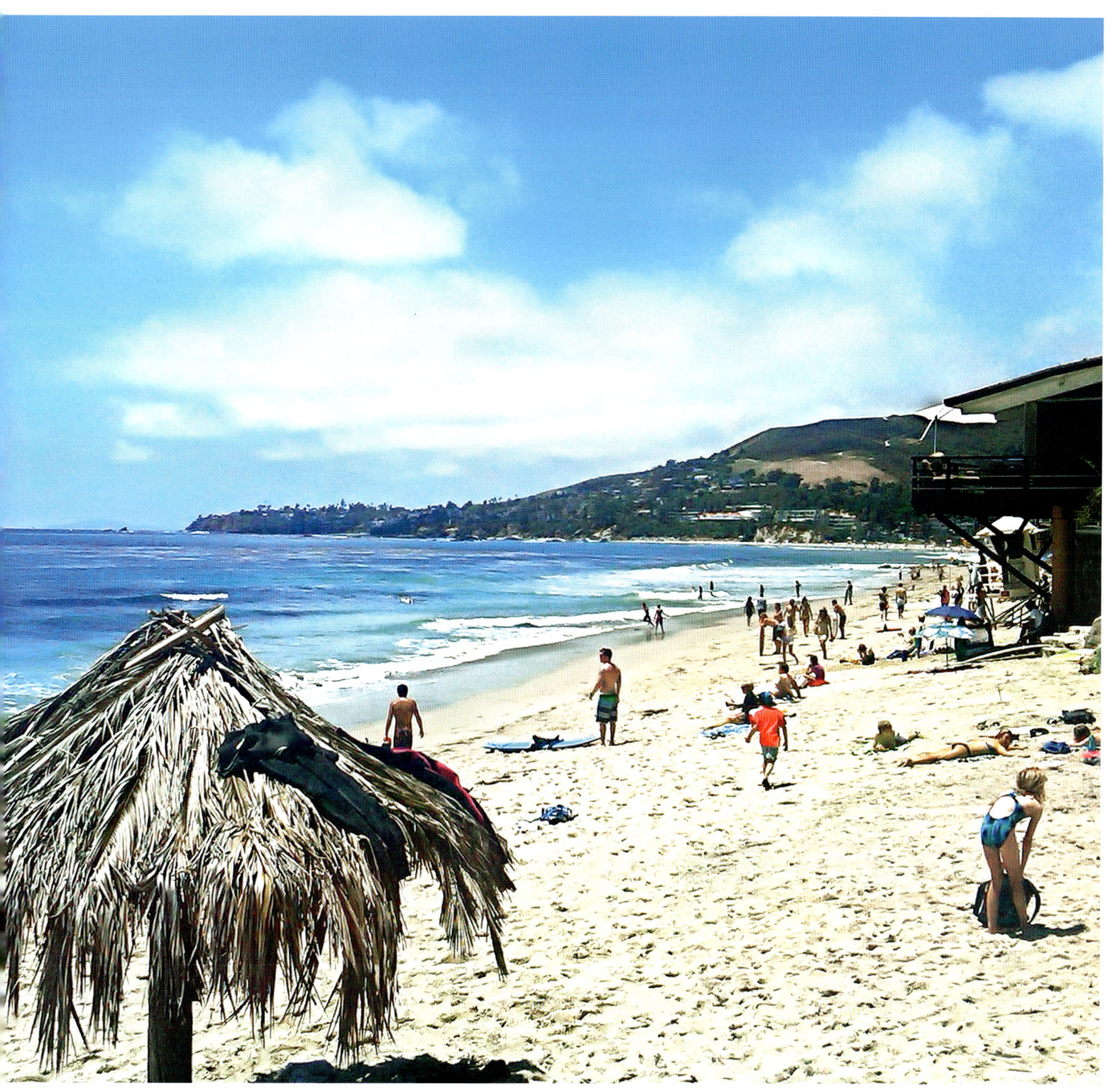

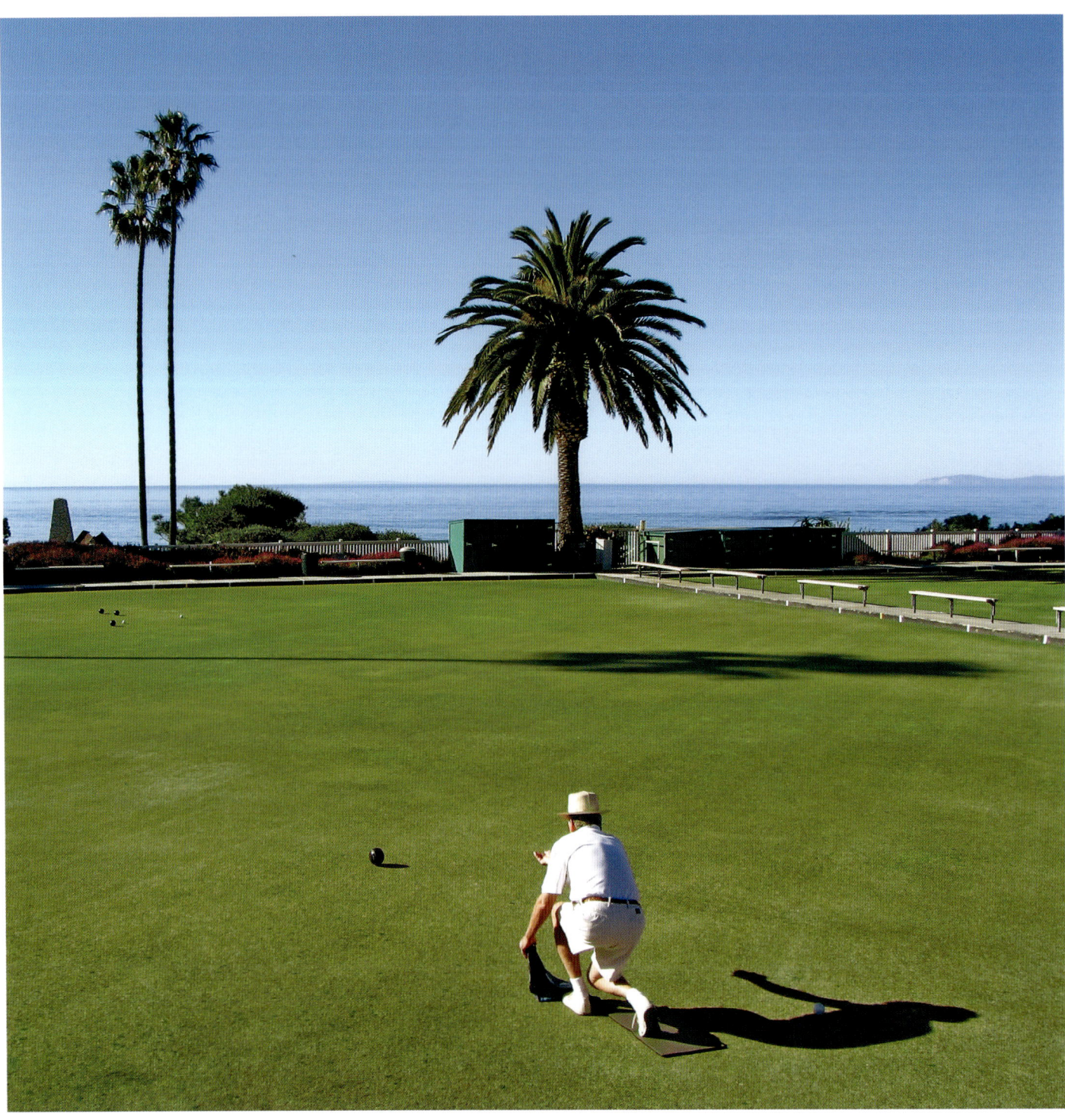

Heisler Park in Spring

Out of a yellow
school bus burst several dozen
second-graders. They
scatter and shout with delight,
glimpsing Divers Cove.
Single file, class, no running–
the teacher's voice is
lost on the spring wind. A lawn
bowler adjusts his
hat, cups the ball in his hands;
then, genuflecting, rolls it.

Green Glass

A sea of green glass.
Secret caves. Dolphins! Why not
a nymph and goblin?

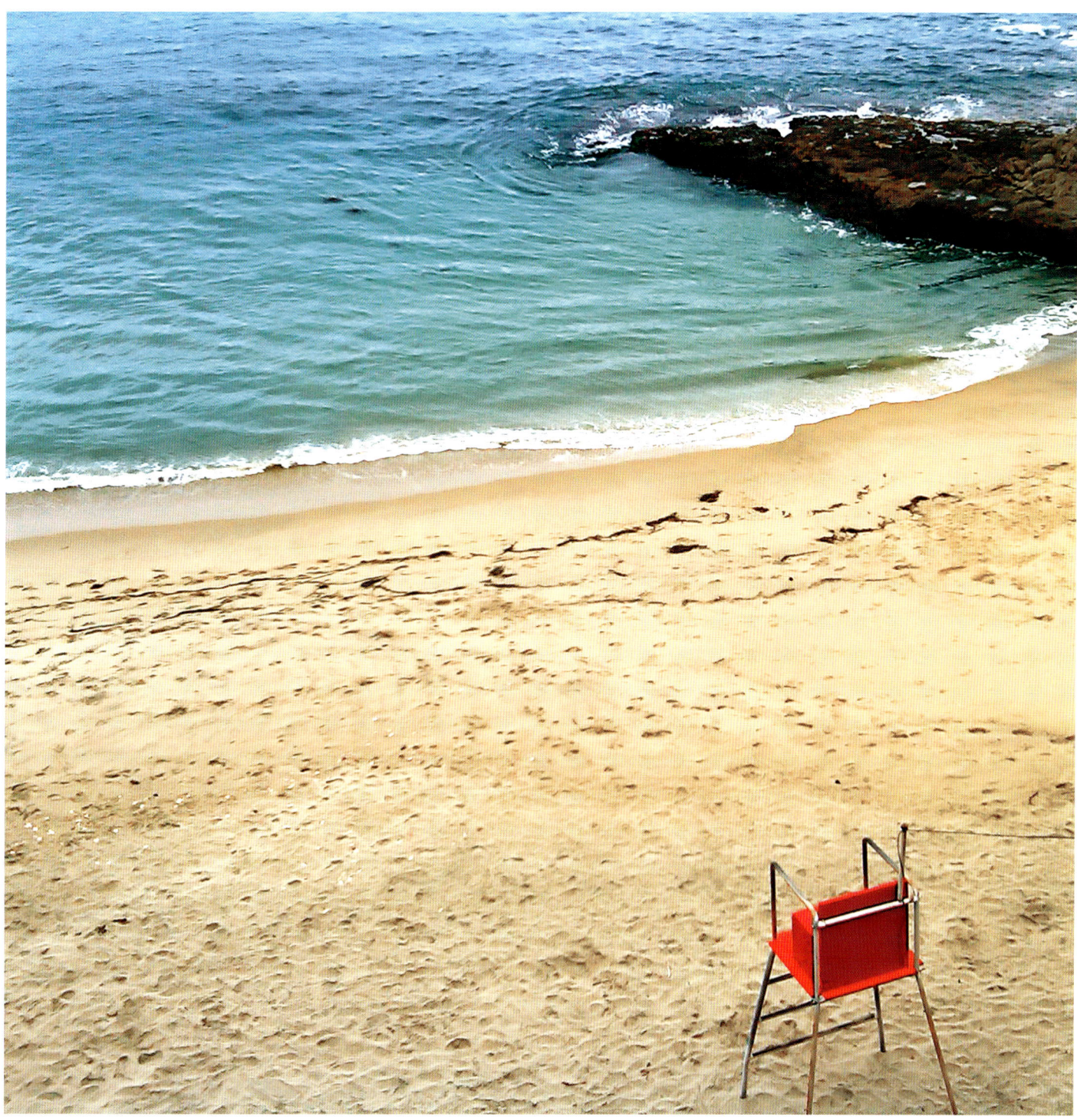

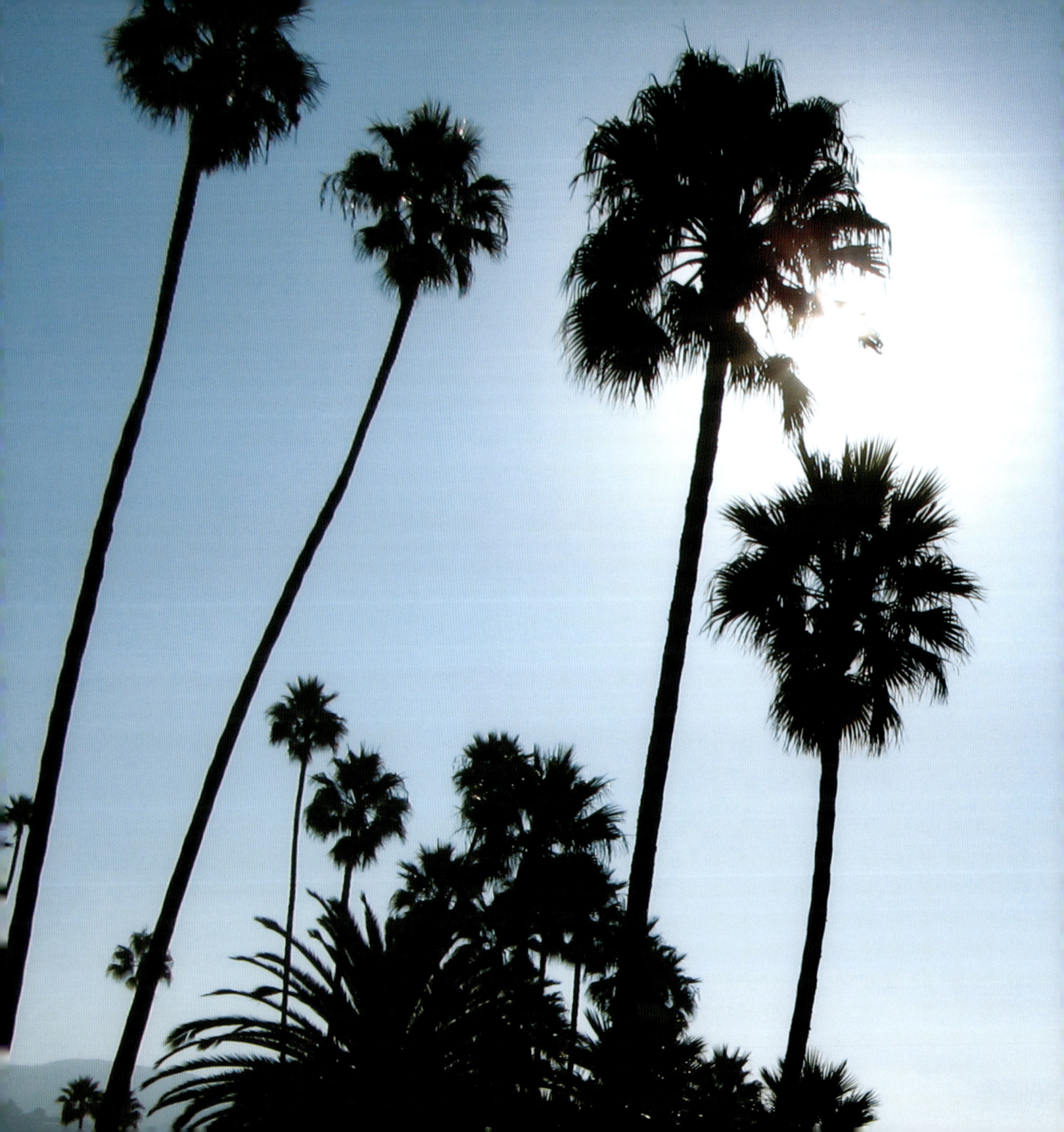

Day's End

as I travel north
the fiery setting sun
is quenched by the sea

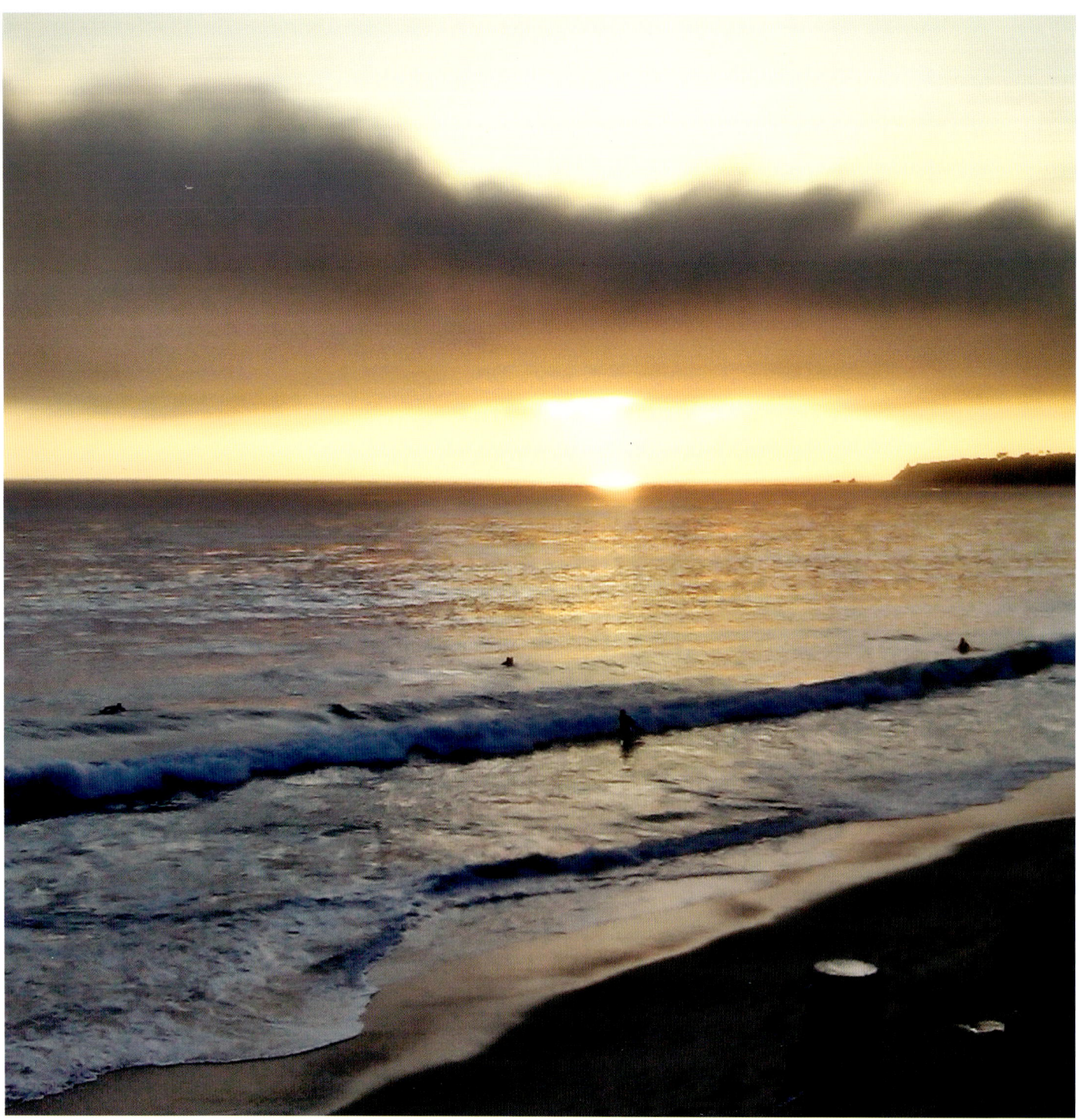

Mystery

I see a surfer
exiting the water. Knee-deep
in the shallows, with the sun
reflecting off his
soaked seal-black wetsuit, he makes
the sign of the cross—
Father, Son, Holy Spirit
—three times, then tucks his
board under his arm and leaves.

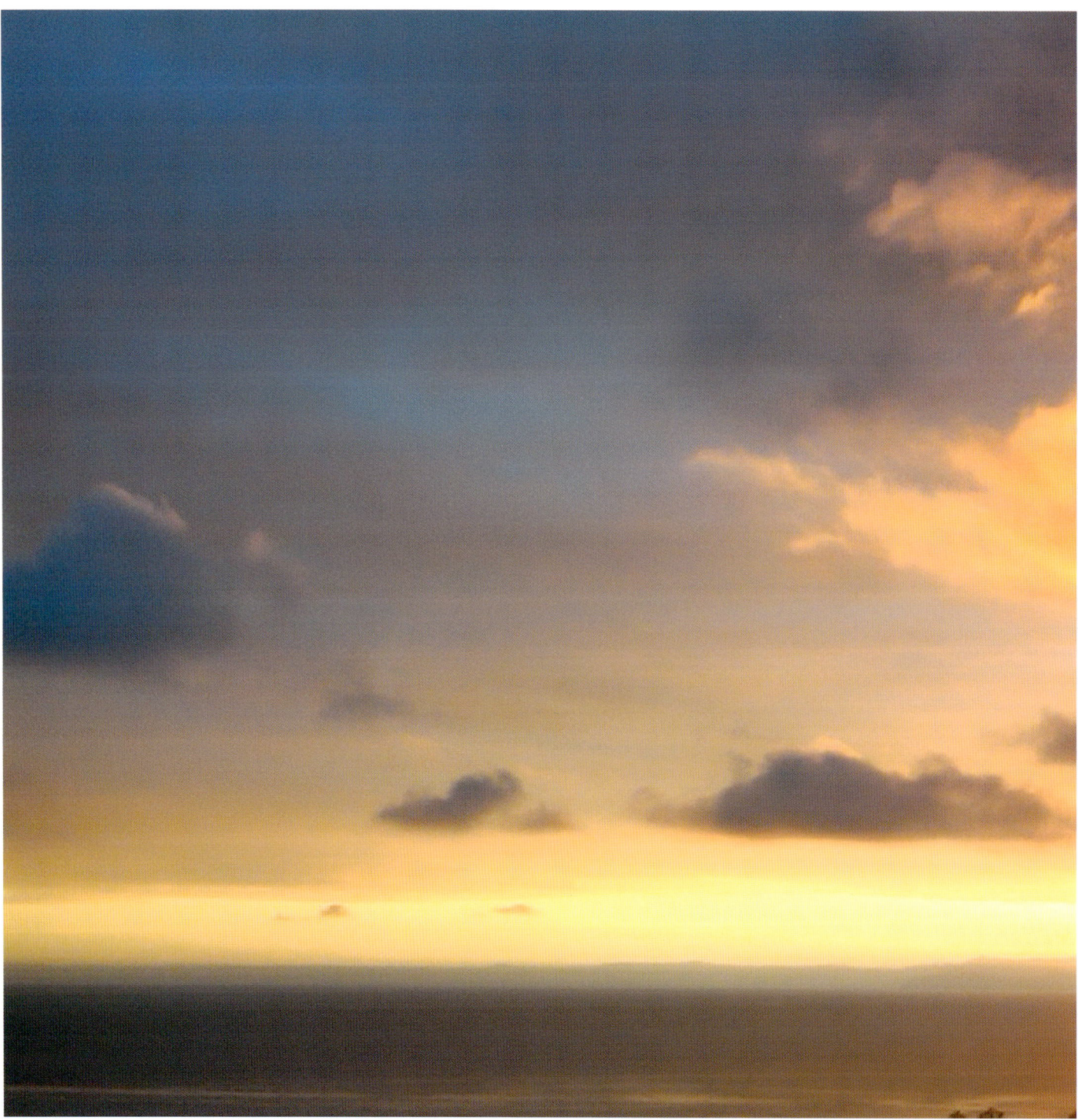

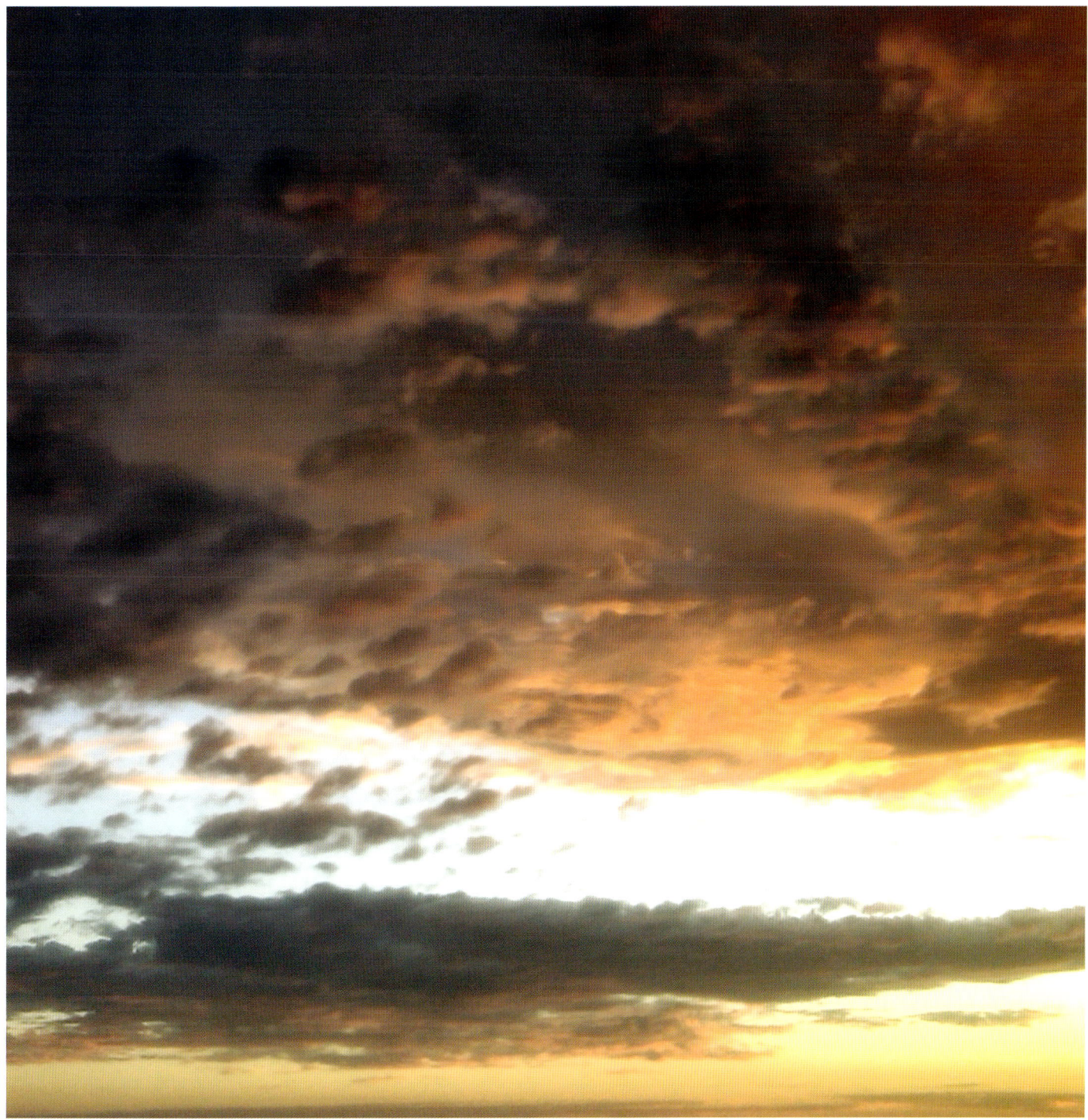

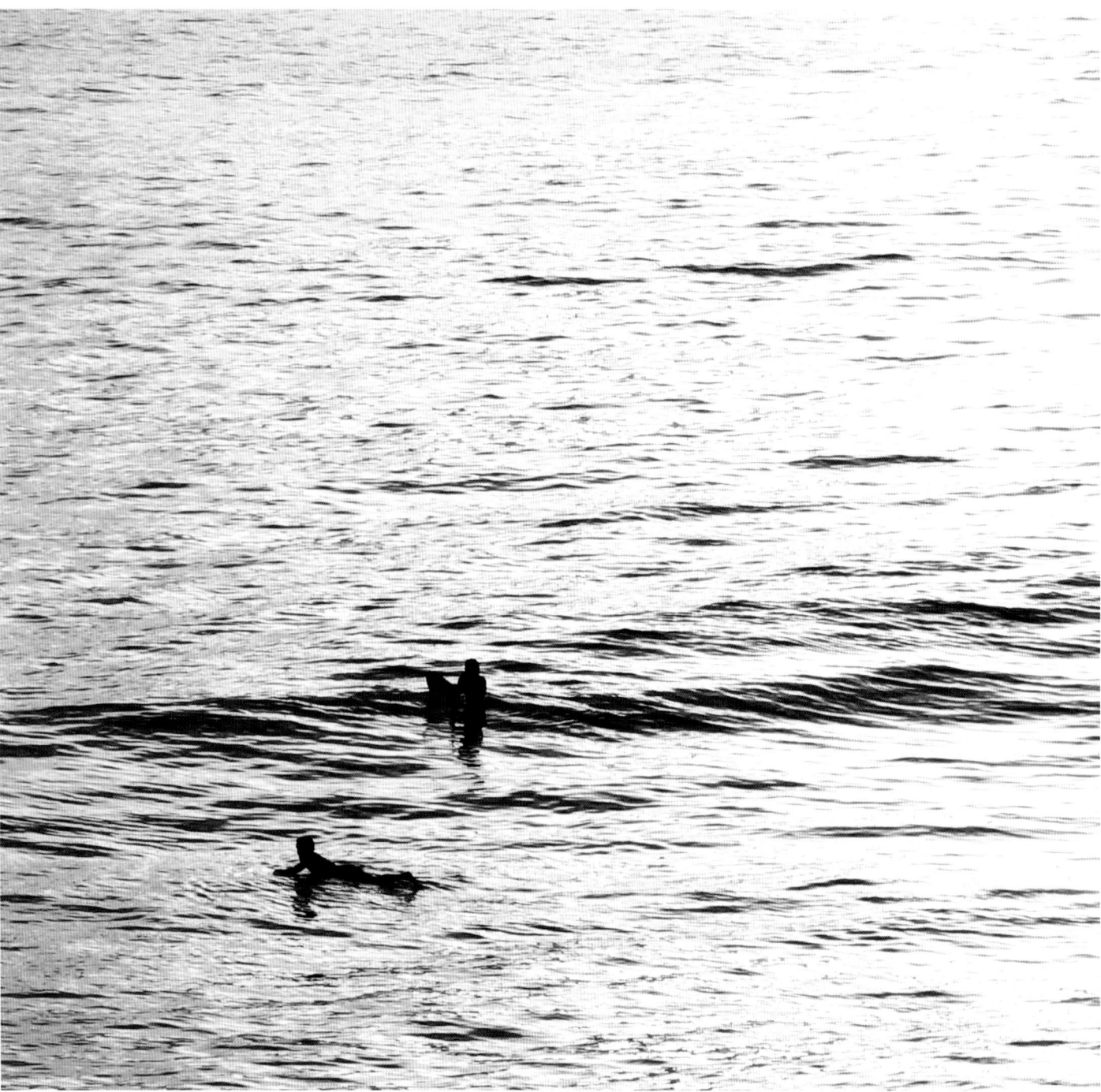

Oak Street Gold

gold spilled from the low-
hanging sun making the sea
gleam like so many black pearls

Laguna Noir

High speed chase, shots fired.
Damp veil hides the horizon
then, afternoon sun.

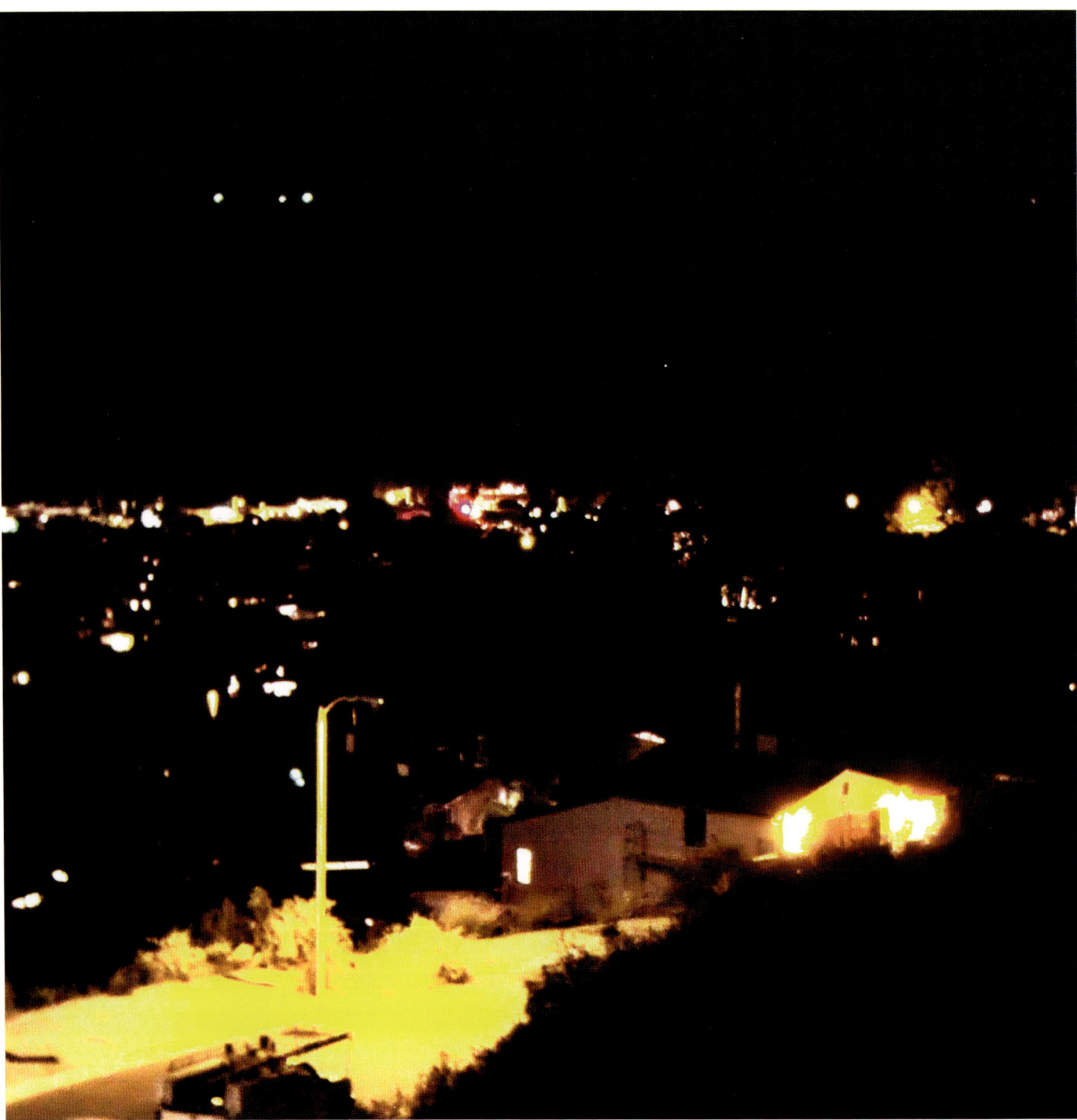

Before Sleep

I lift my head from the pillow
and glimpse the almost-full moon
and its reflection on the ocean—
a broad, golden path to the horizon.
A red traffic light
at Cress Street and Pacific Coast Highway
turns green.
The streetlights and illuminated houses
blur together into a twinkling haze.
I close my eyes and sleep.

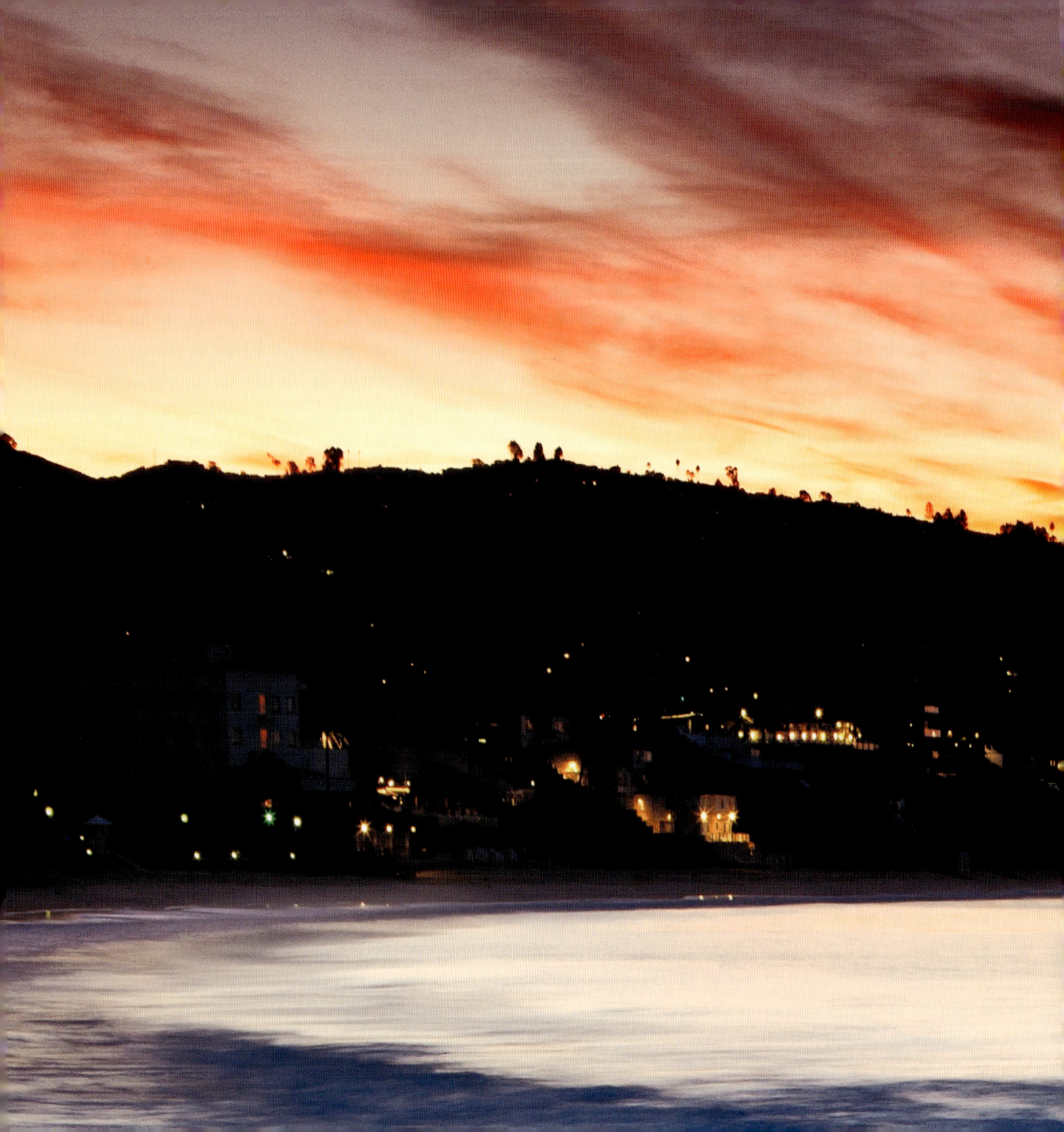

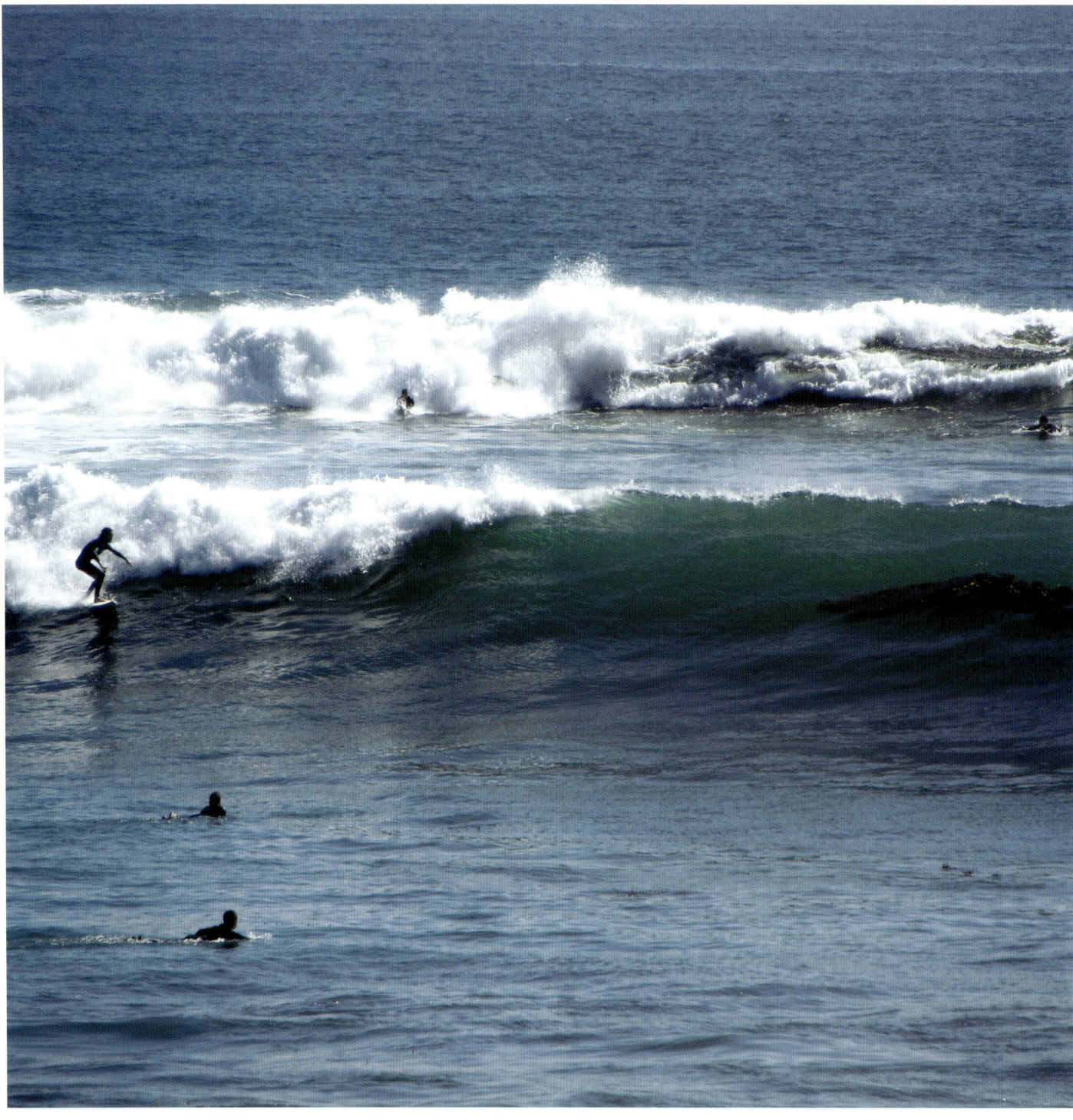

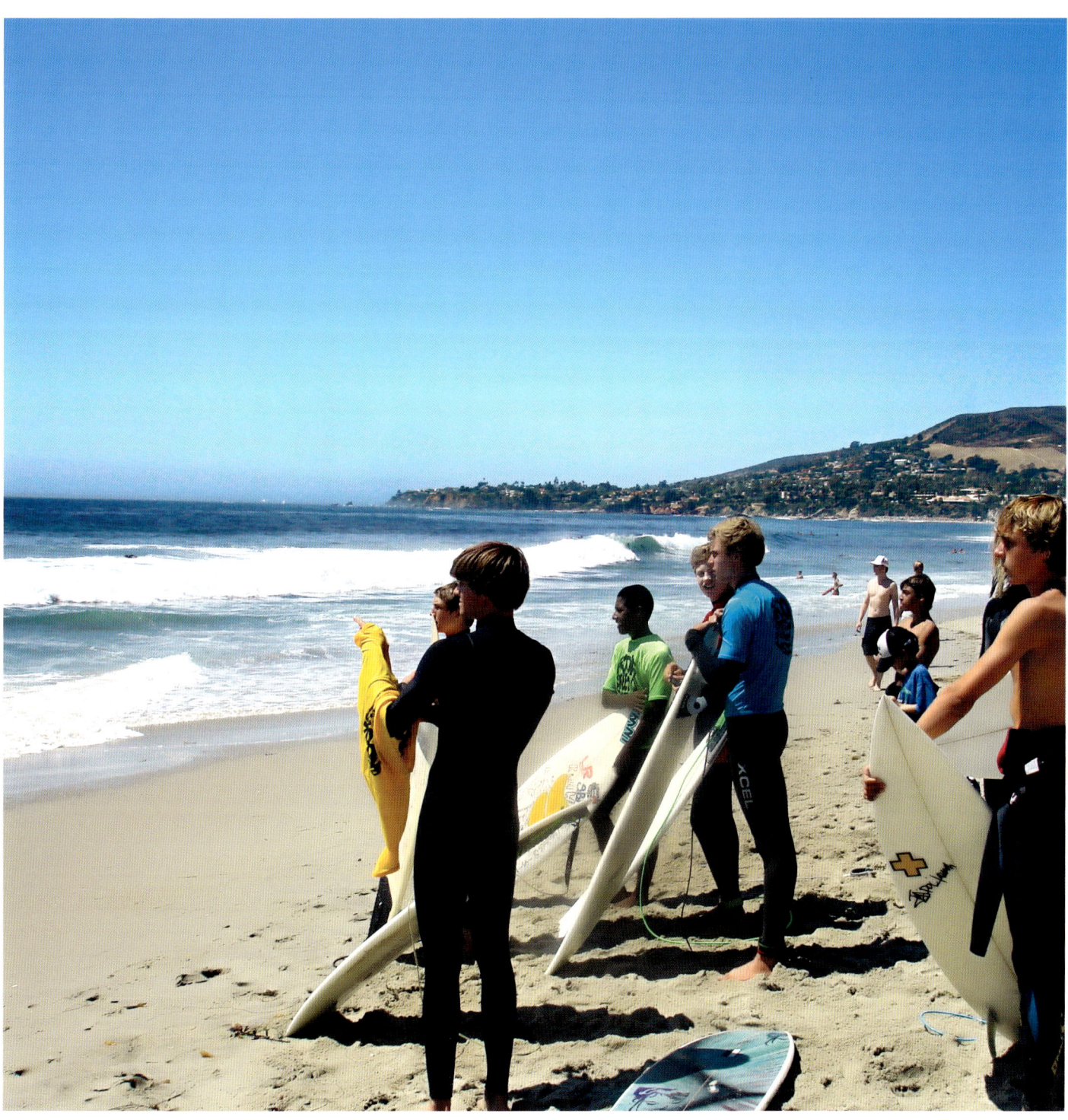

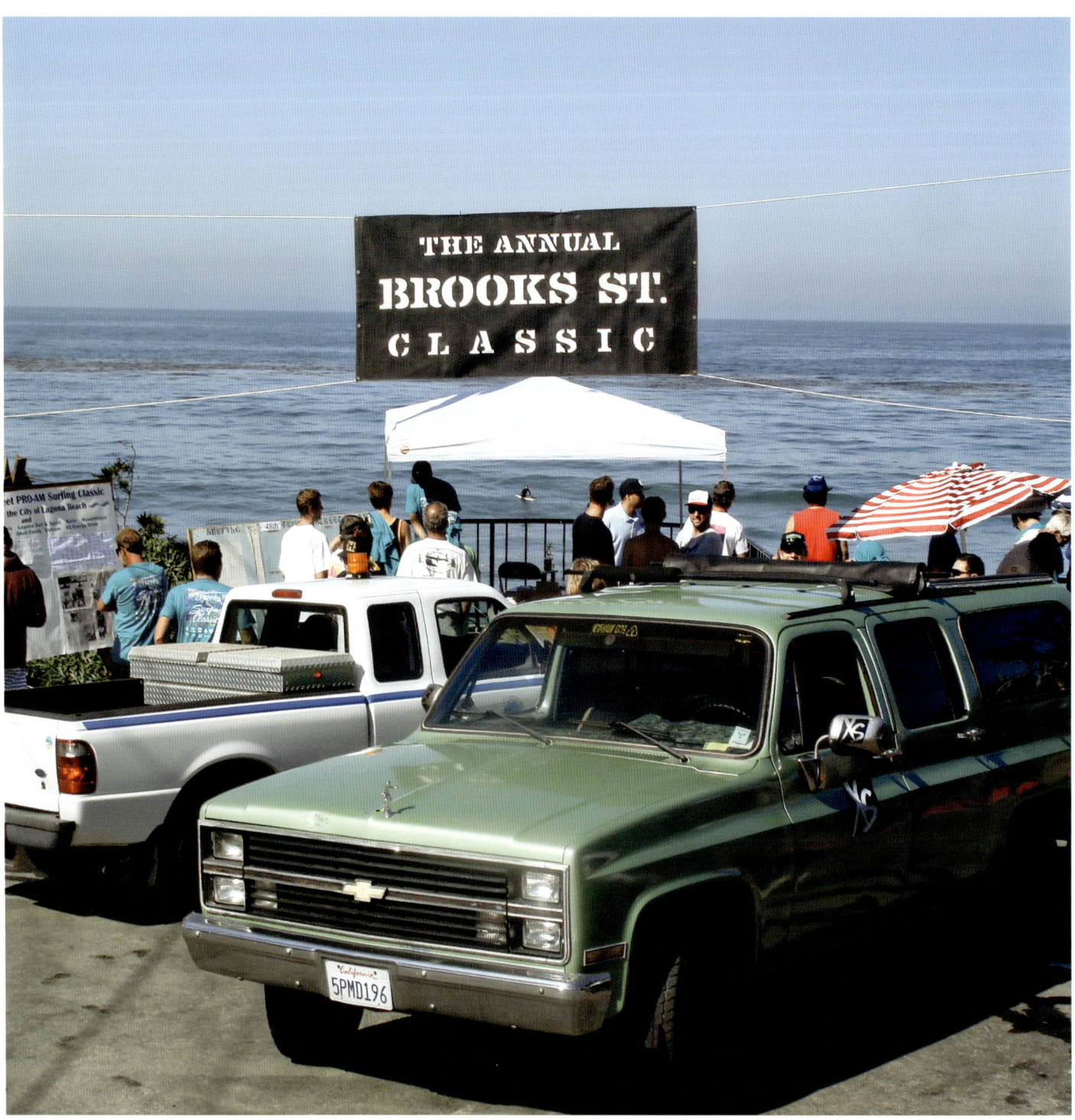

It's On!

A south swell arrives;
locals converge on Brooks Street.
Let the show begin!

Sli-Dog's Surf Camp

Aqua Hakama.
Party waves and sand castles.
Adolfo's tacos,
Gina's pizza, and candy
aplenty from Circle K.
Reapply sunscreen,
and repeat.

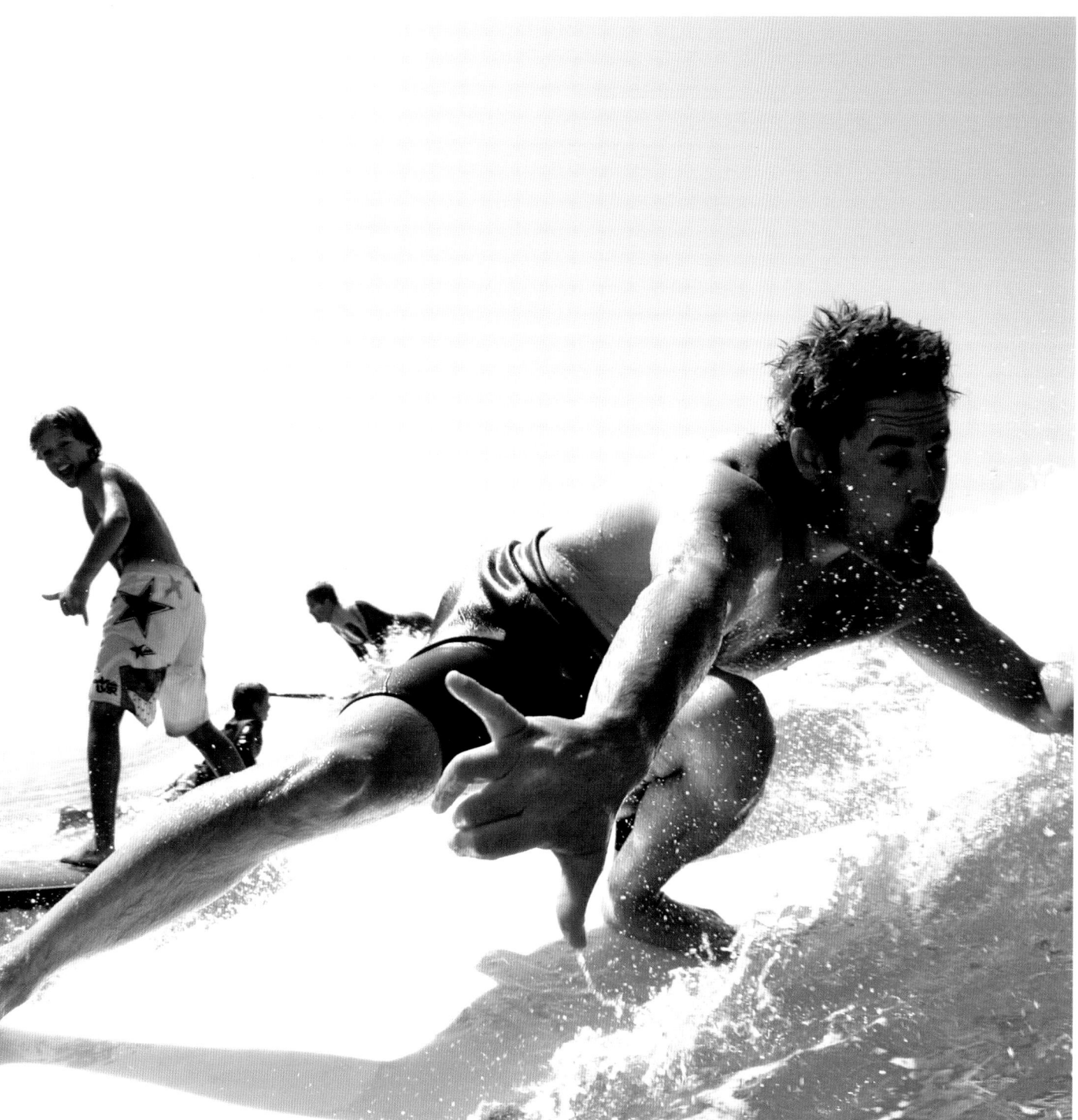

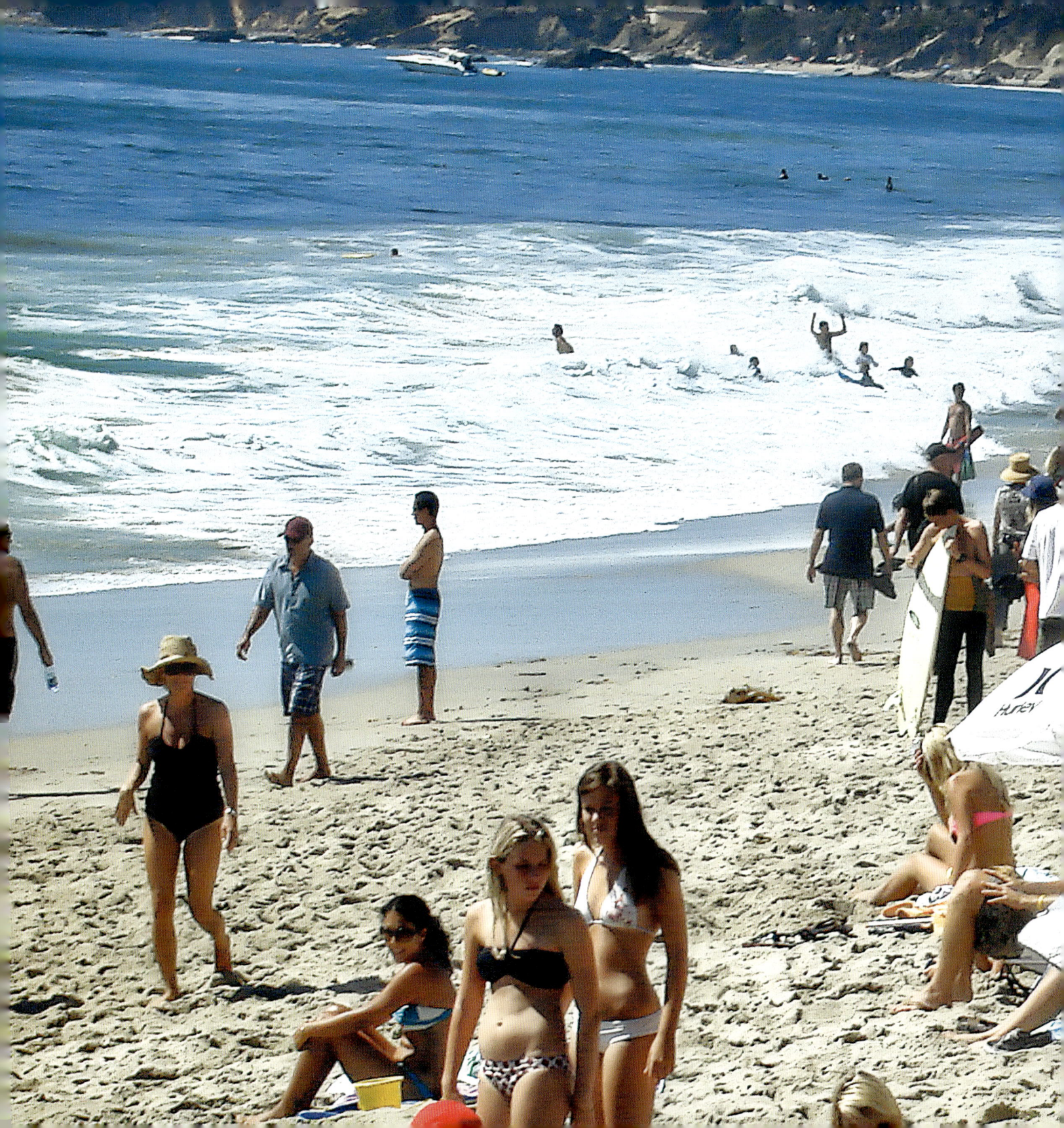

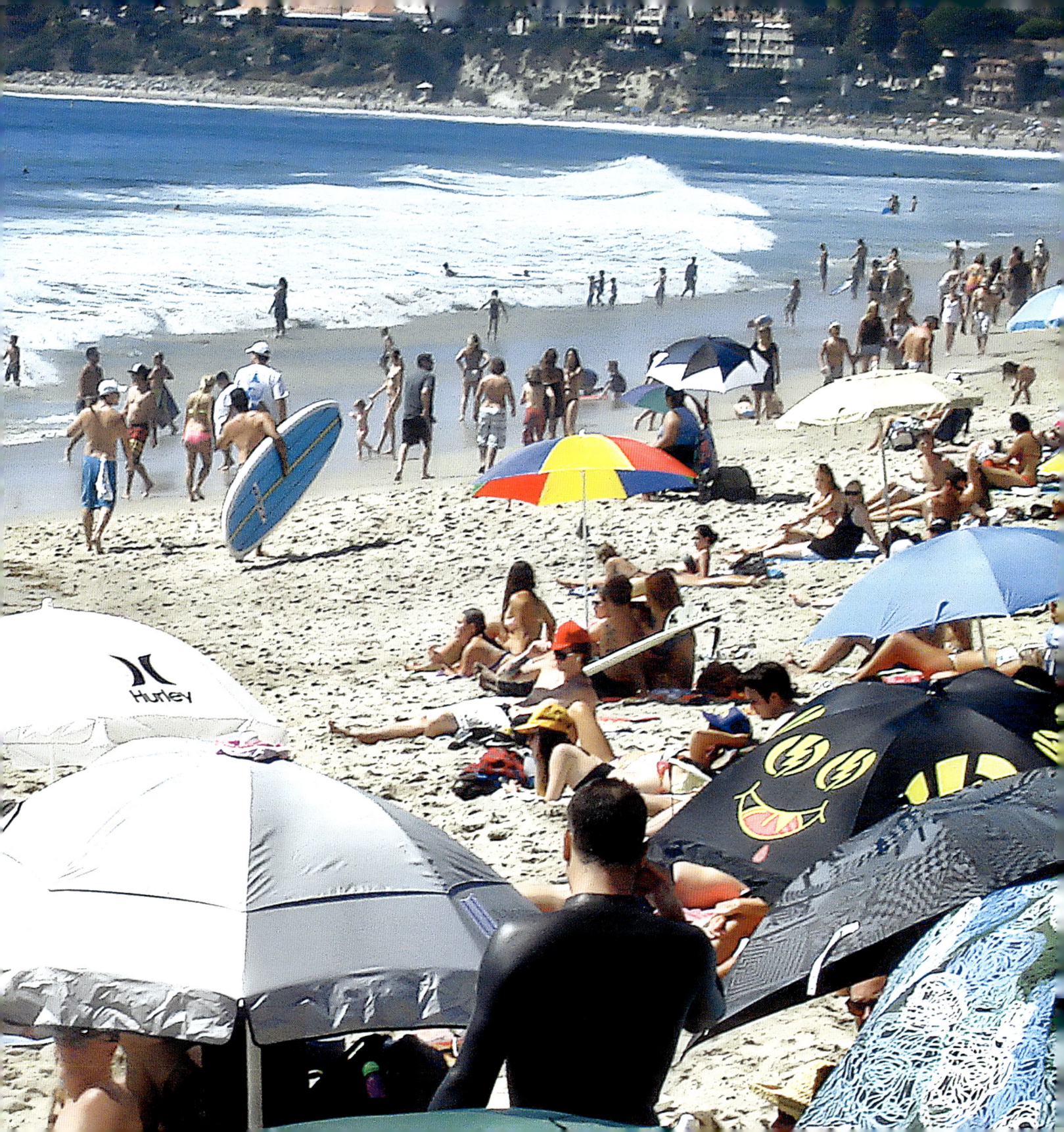

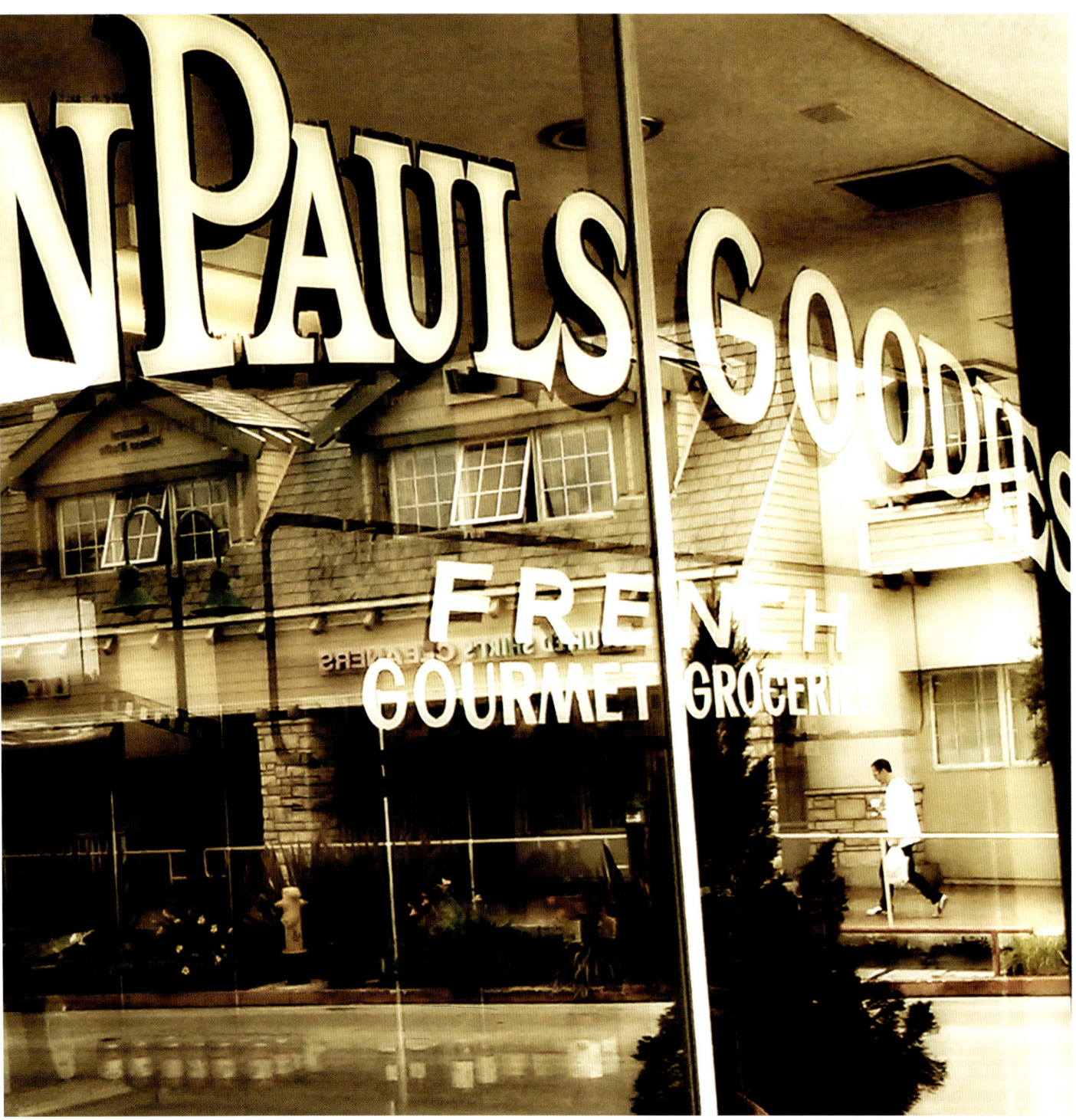

Fear and Trembling... and the Best Coffee

I parked between the lines
and not too close to the door,
because he hates the smell of exhaust.
I approached the Frenchman
warily
taking care not to make direct eye contact
or any sudden moves
or political statements.
I put three-fifty on the counter—
the price has gone up—
and escaped with my coffee,

unscathed.

It was delicious.

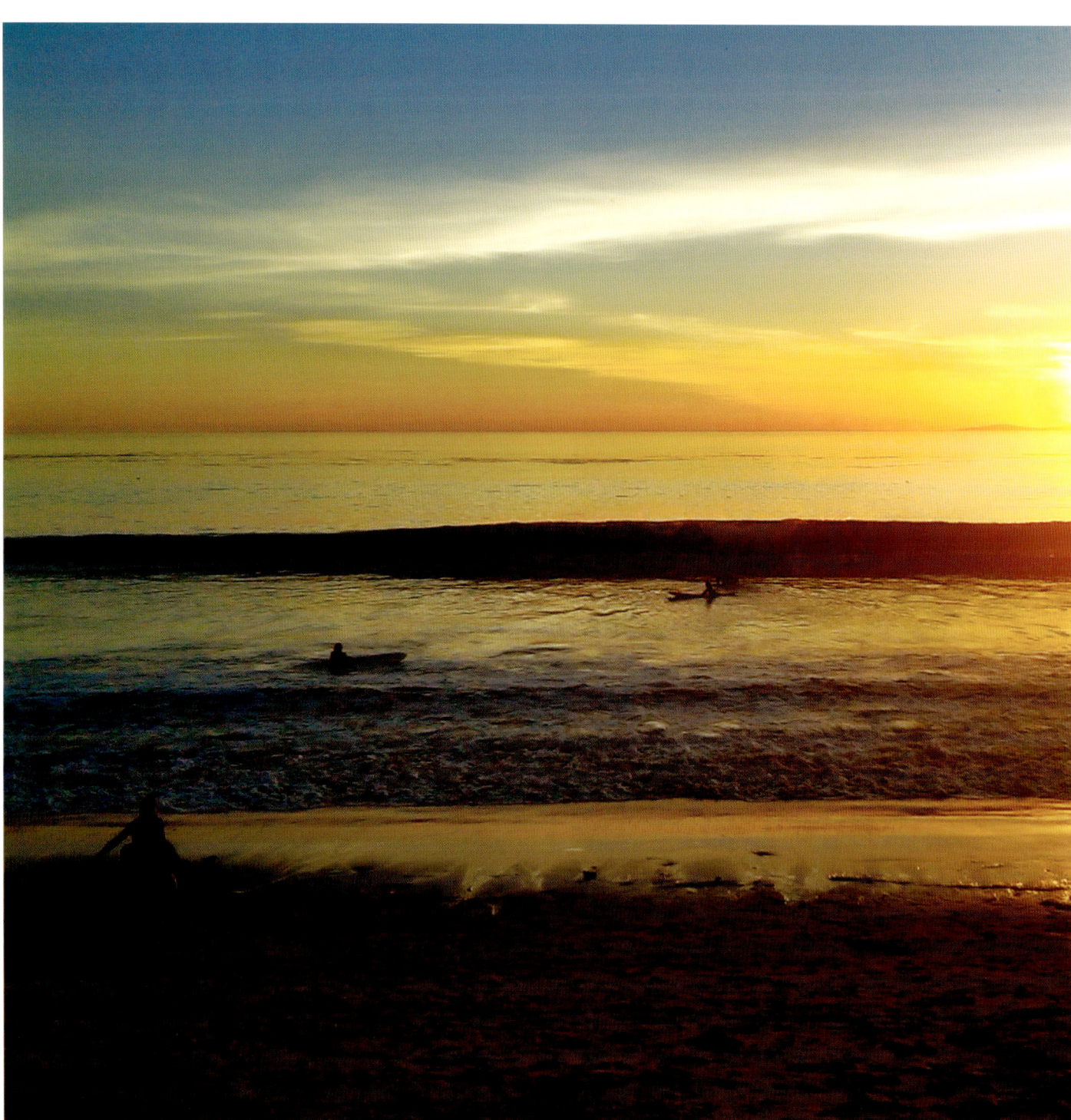

November Glass

Gold November glass—
one more wave, then another.
The sun flares, then fades.

Coyotes

As night falls
and the houses on the hill light up
one by one
the coyotes call
to each other across the canyon,
mournful howls
then short yips and yaps
building to a frenzied clamor.
I can't remember exactly how they hunt
or organize themselves
and wonder
if this is a call to a feast of rabbit or neighborhood cat
or a sound of warning
or a declaration on behalf of Nature
that she is holding her ground.

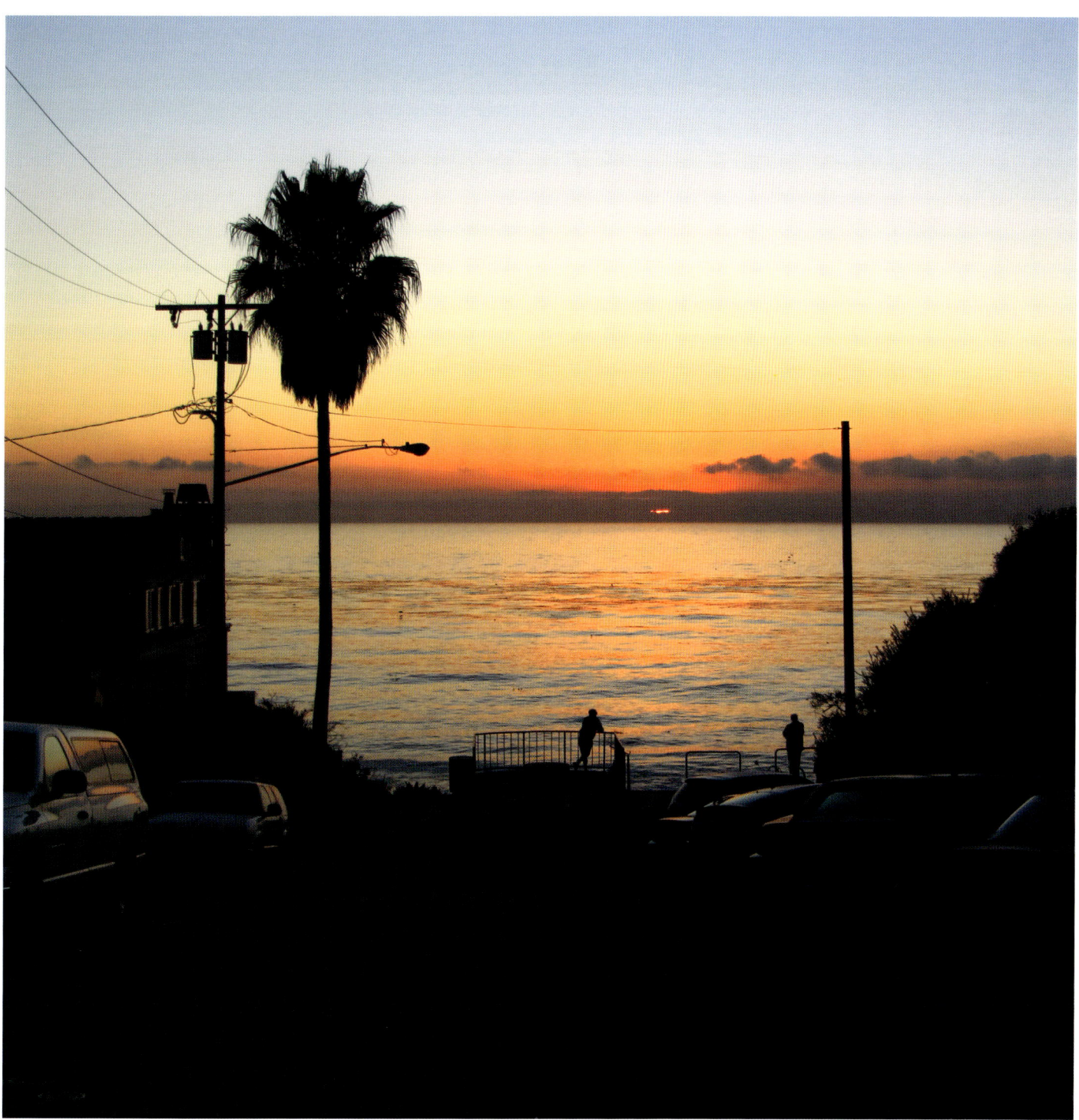

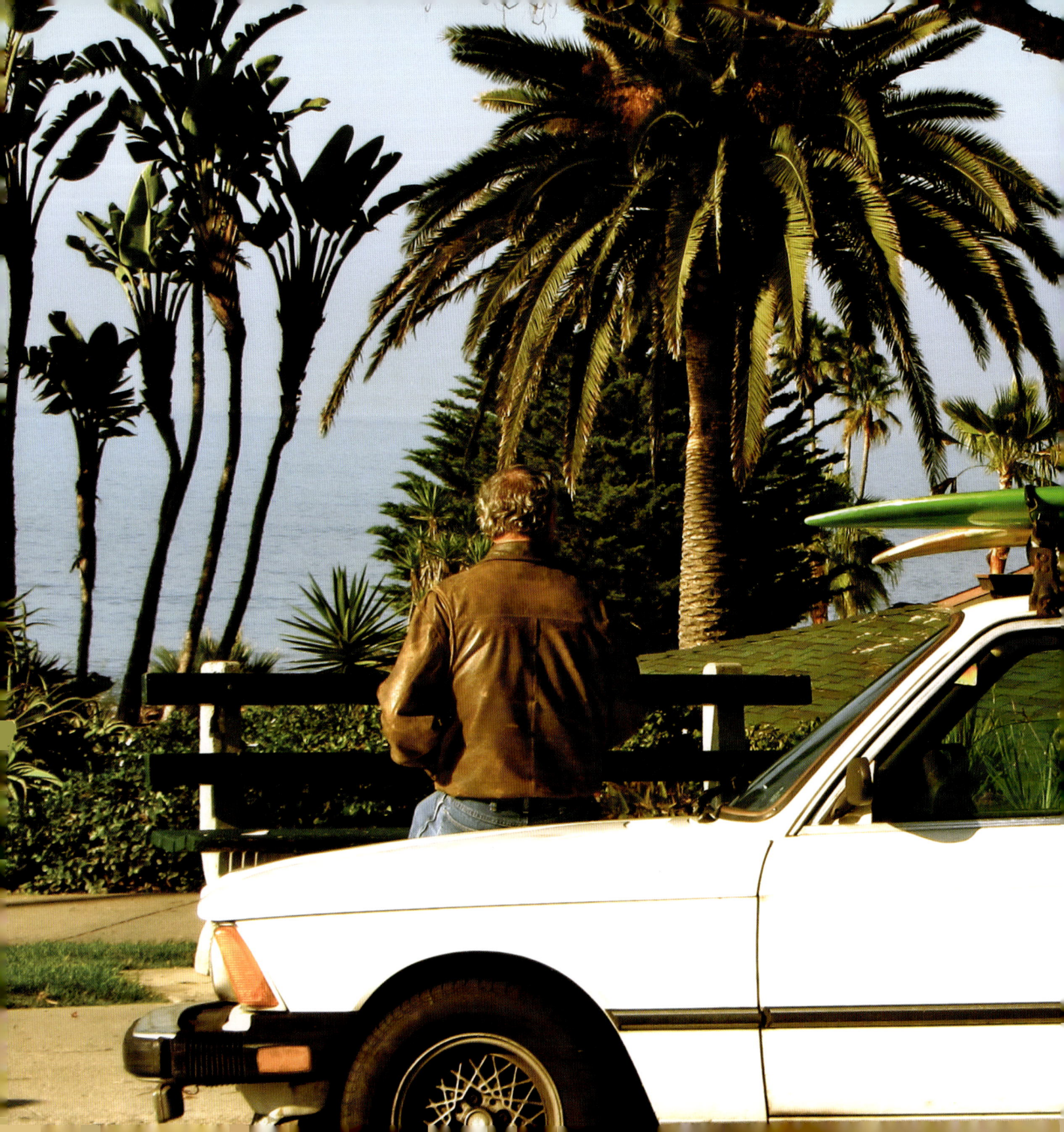

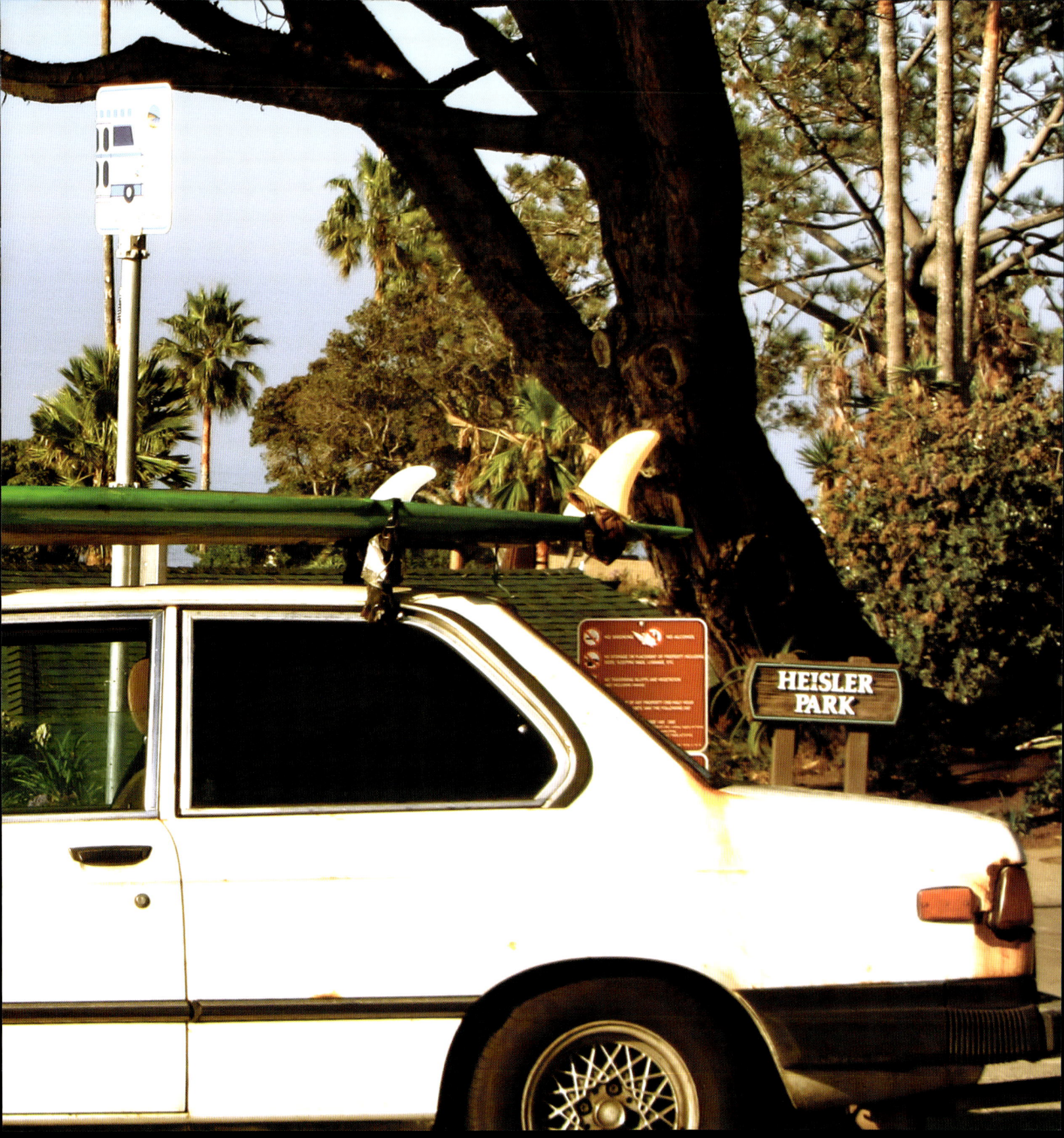

Plein Air

A woman in a broad-brimmed straw hat
gray hair tied back
looks out at the ocean
then lightly, quickly
brushes paint on a canvas
daubing at Main Beach
defining the reef at Brooks Street
giving shape to headlands farther south.

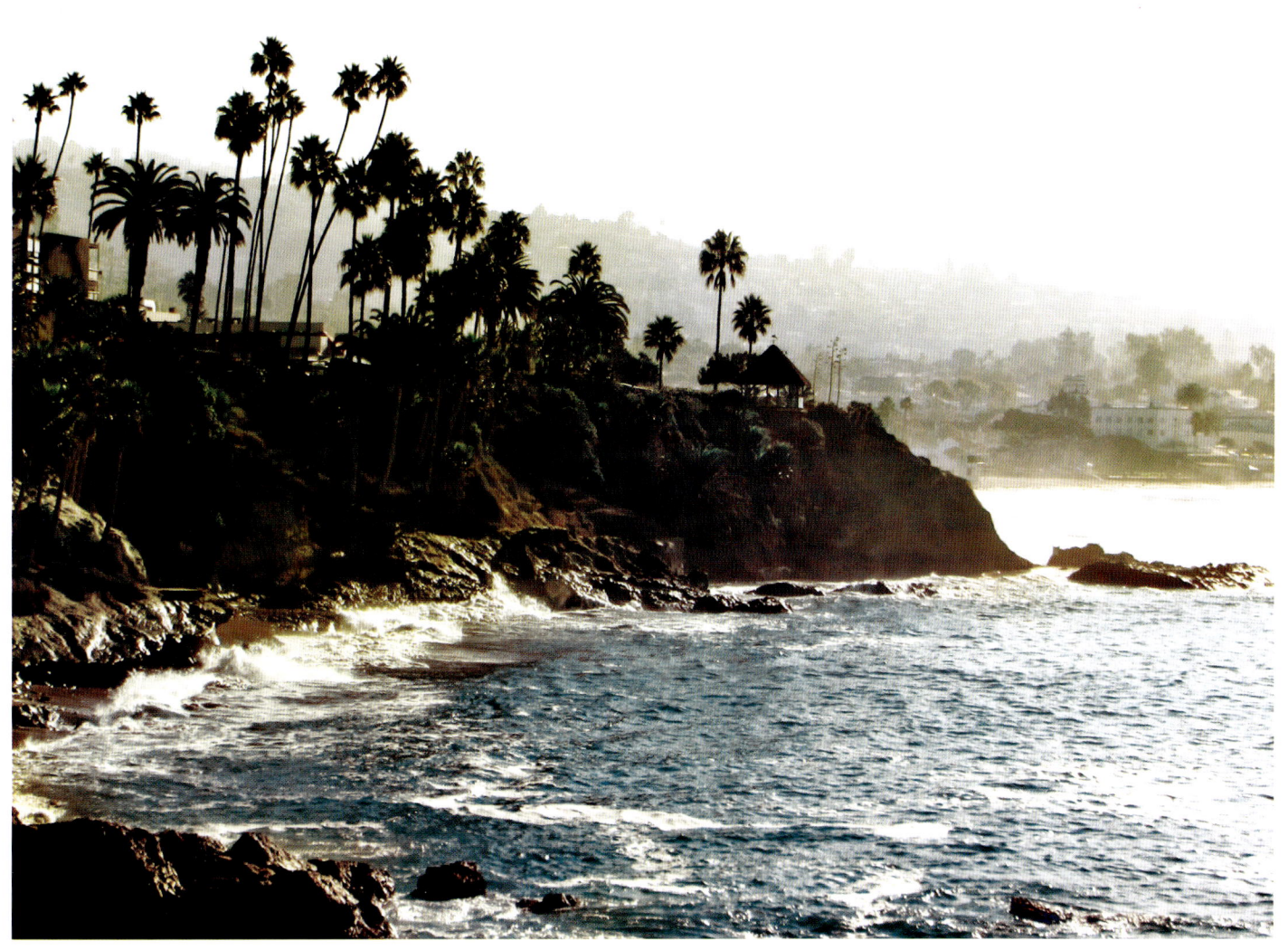

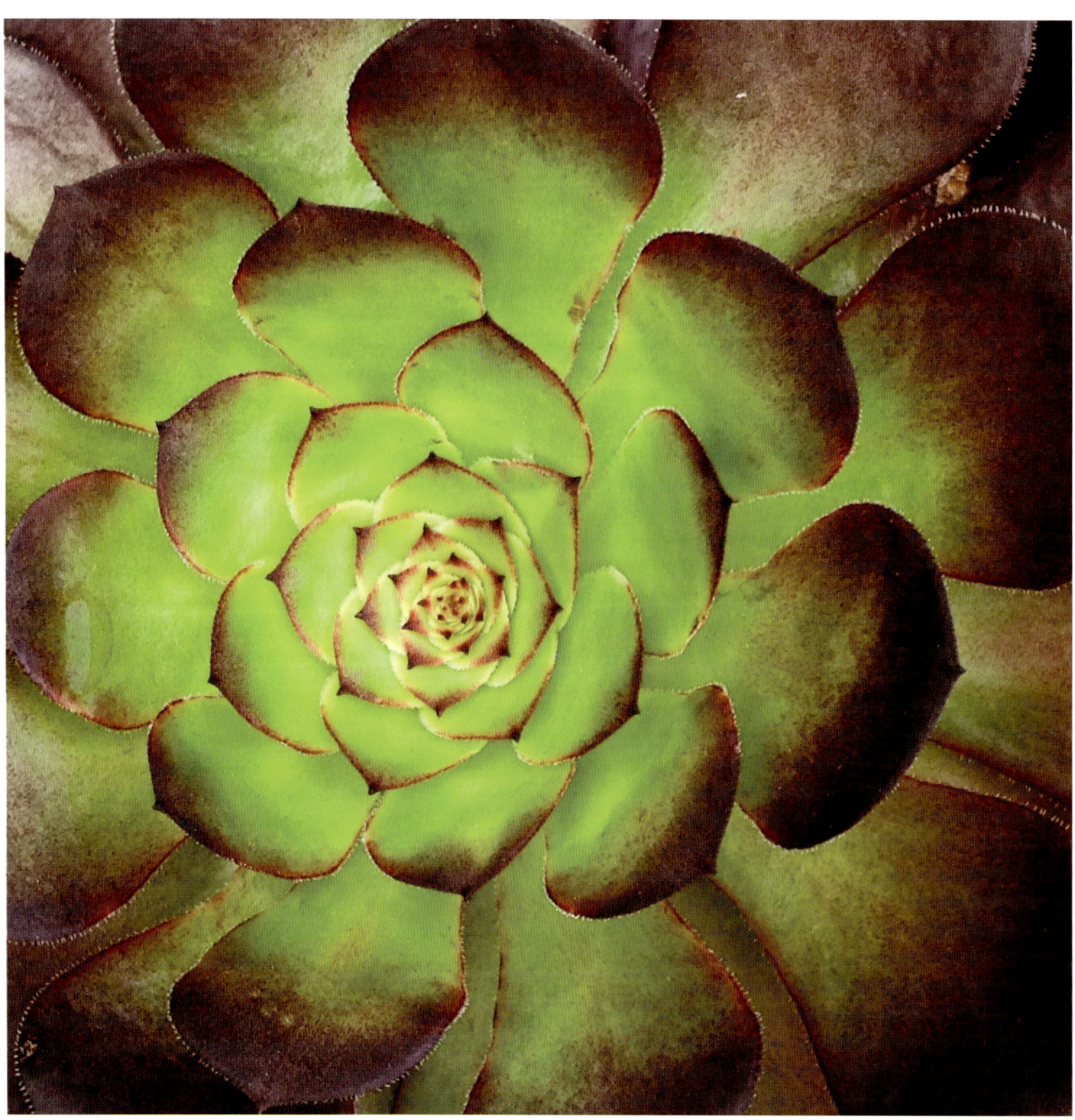

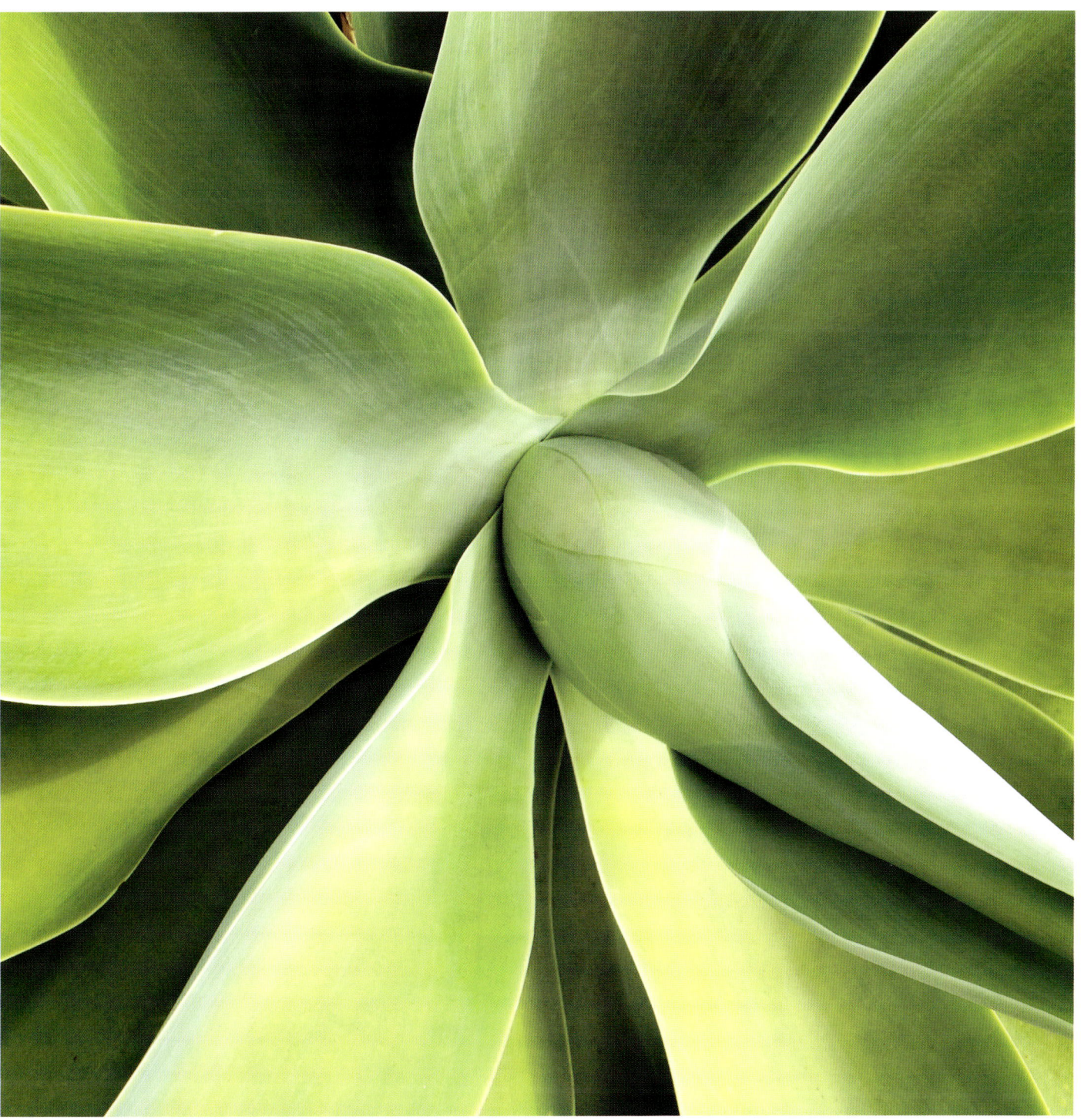

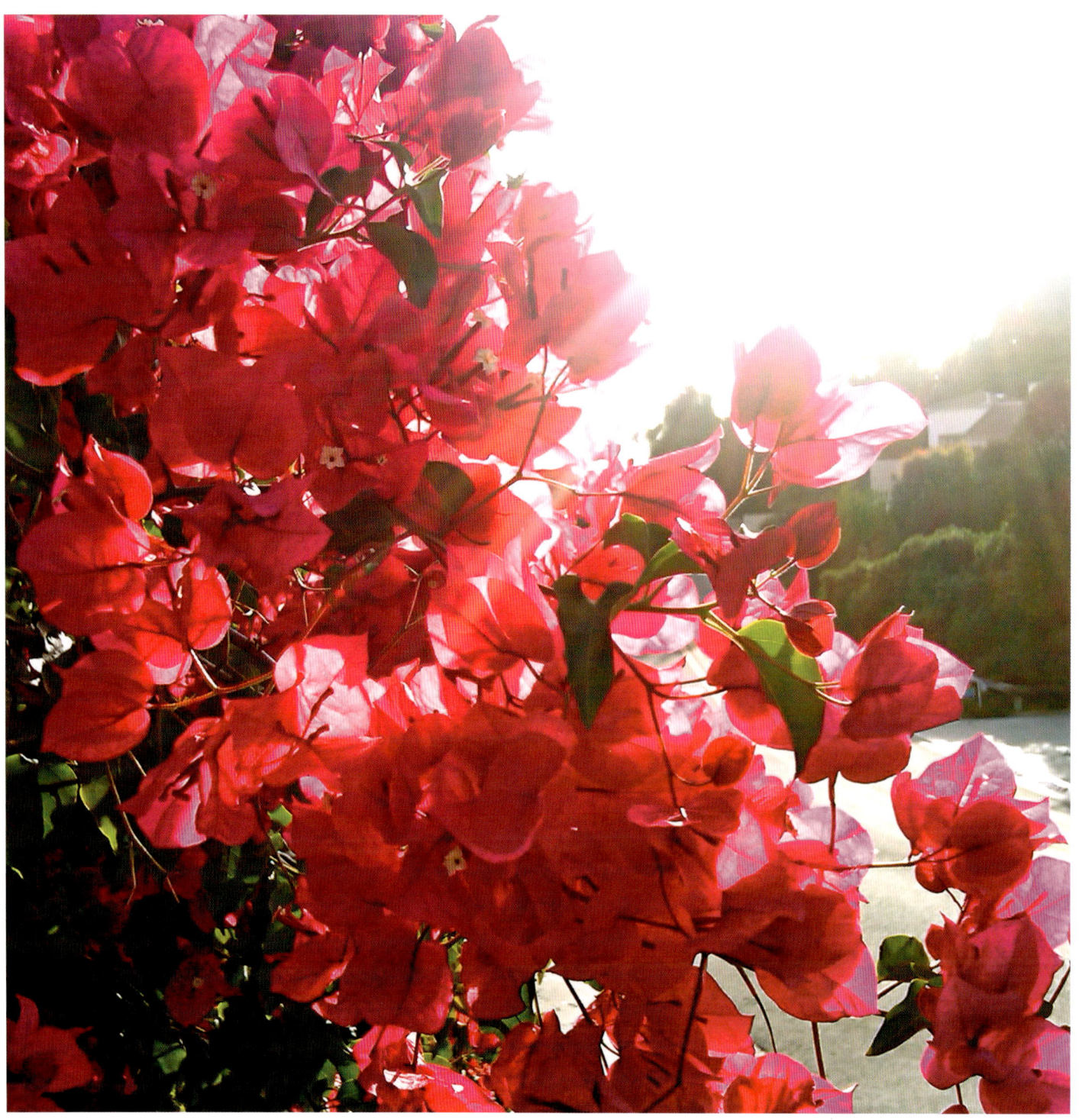

Bougainvillea

The magenta vine
climbs trees, clambers up branches
and shouts, "Look at me!"

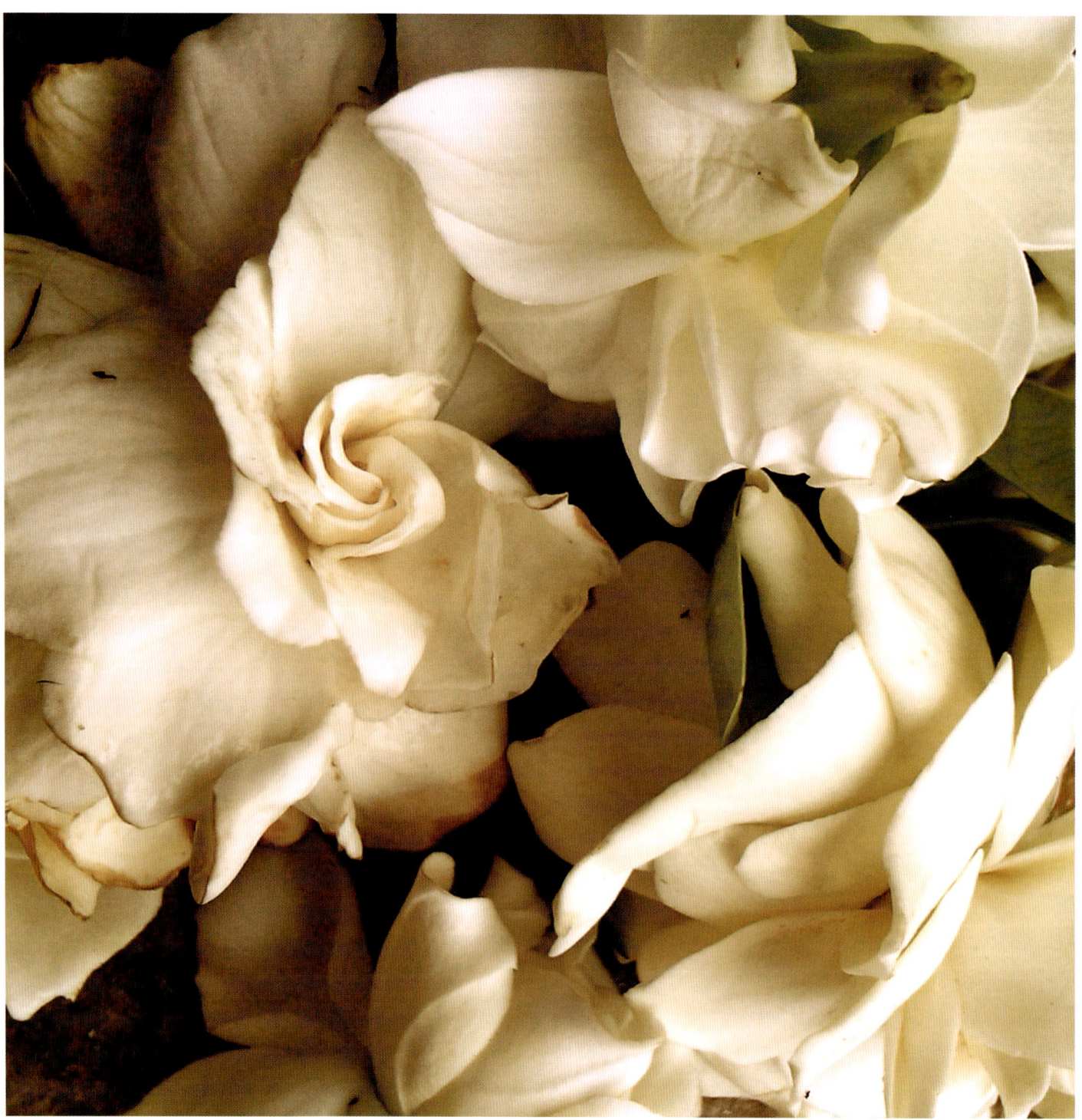

The Good Gardener

Oh!

The good gardener
has been here today
pruning and watering
and he left a
fragrant little jumble
of gardenia and plumeria
blossoms
on the doorstep

Aloe

green, red, soft, spiky
medicinal, beautiful
leaves that wound and heal

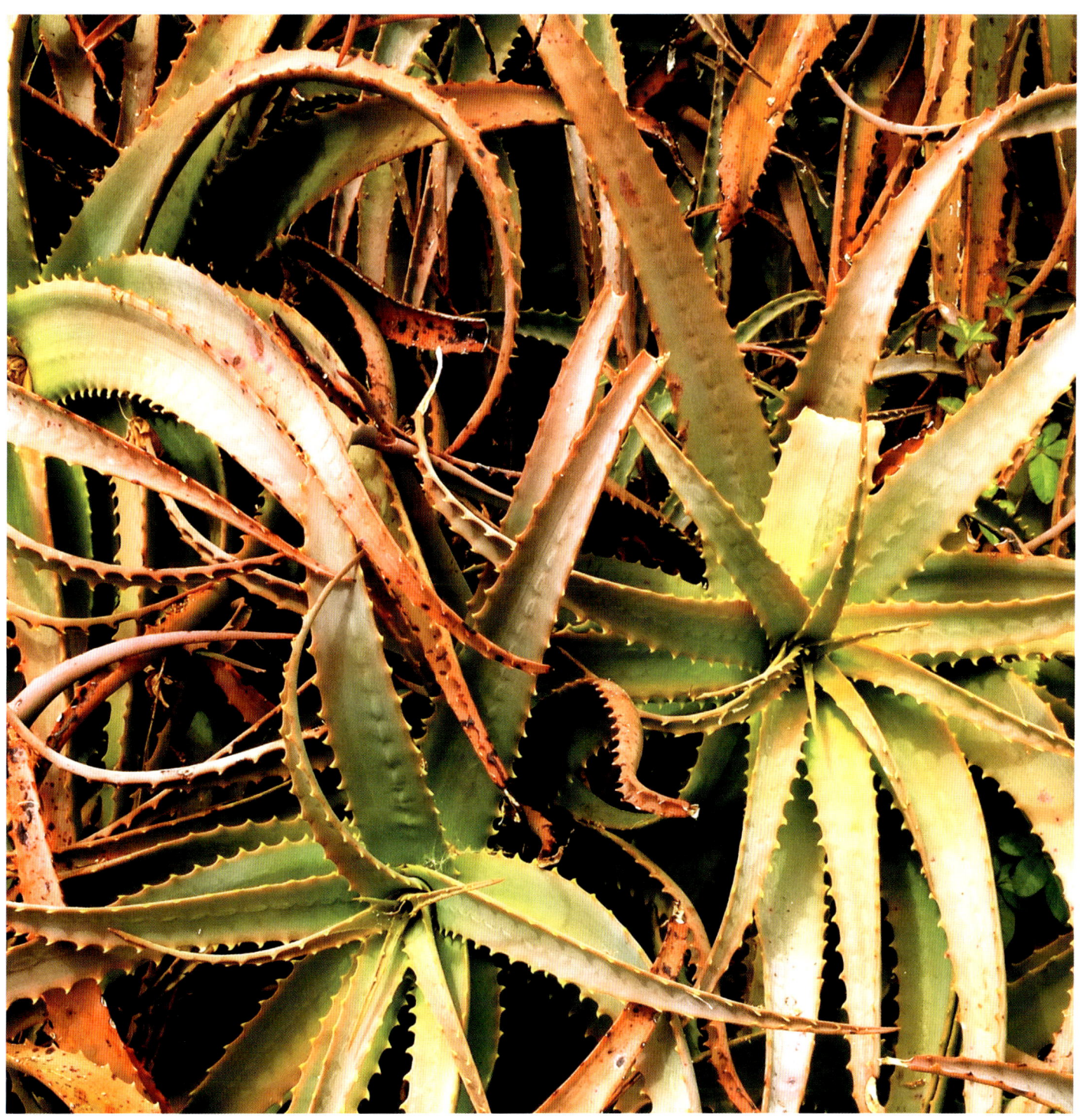

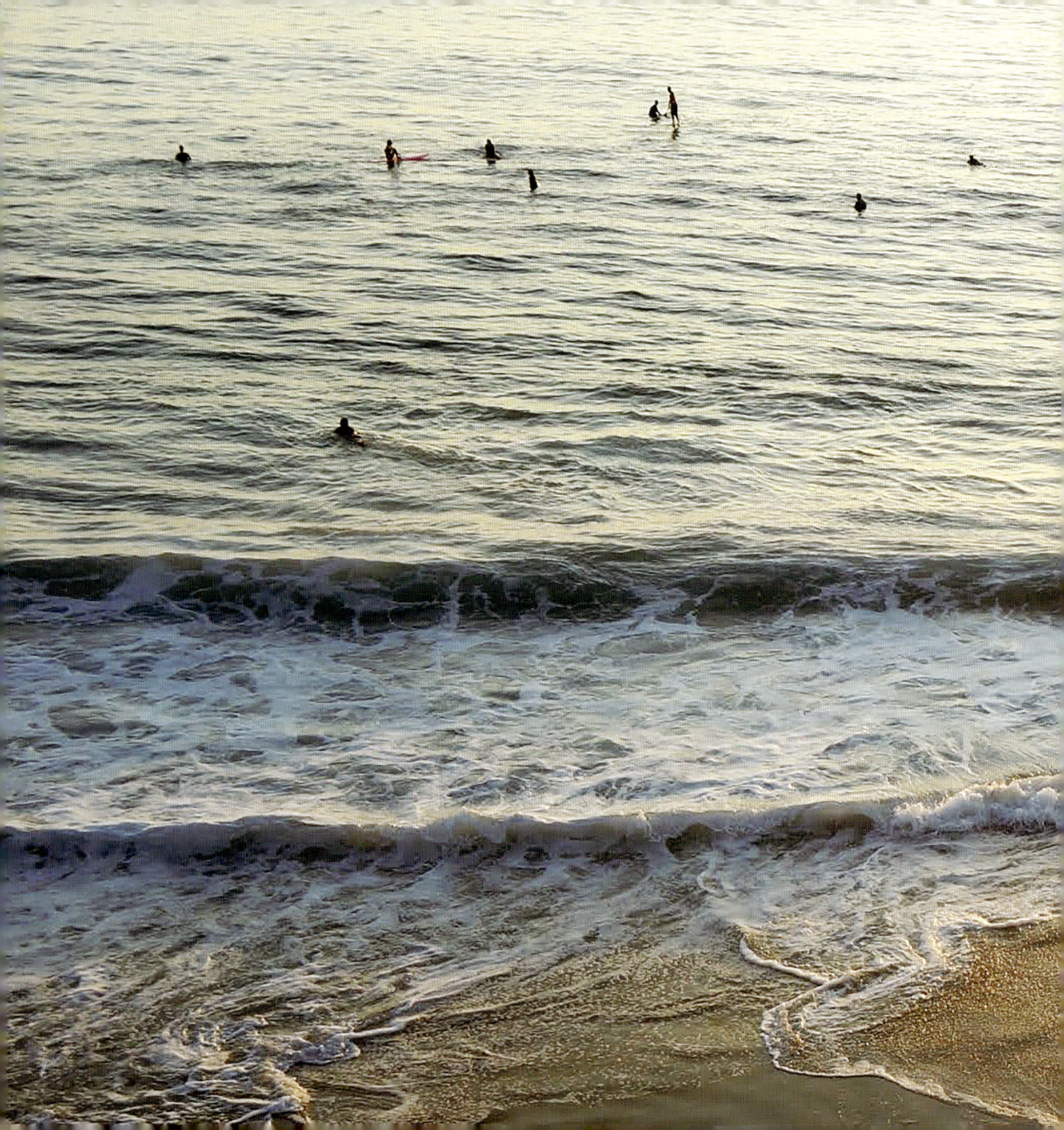

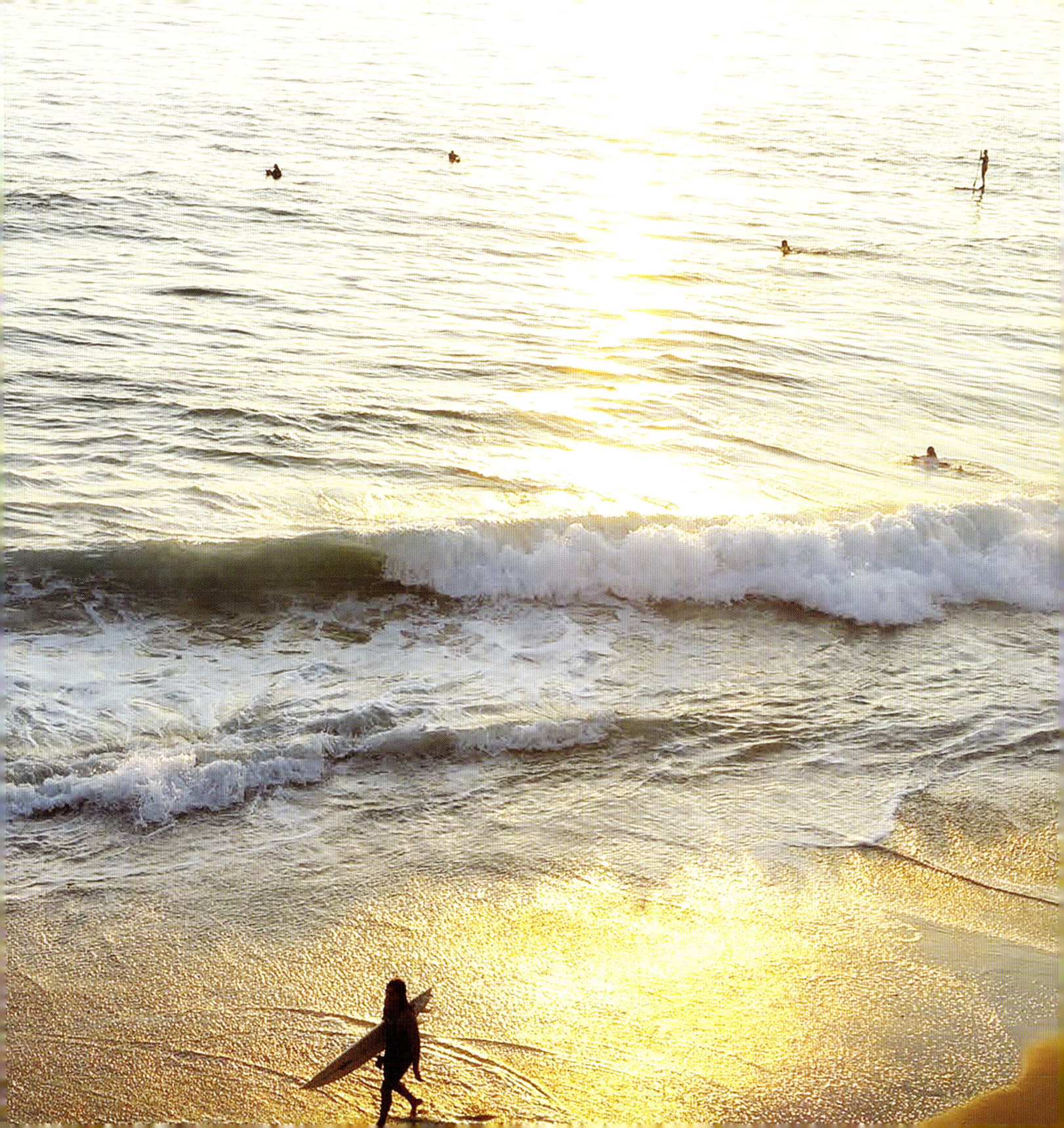

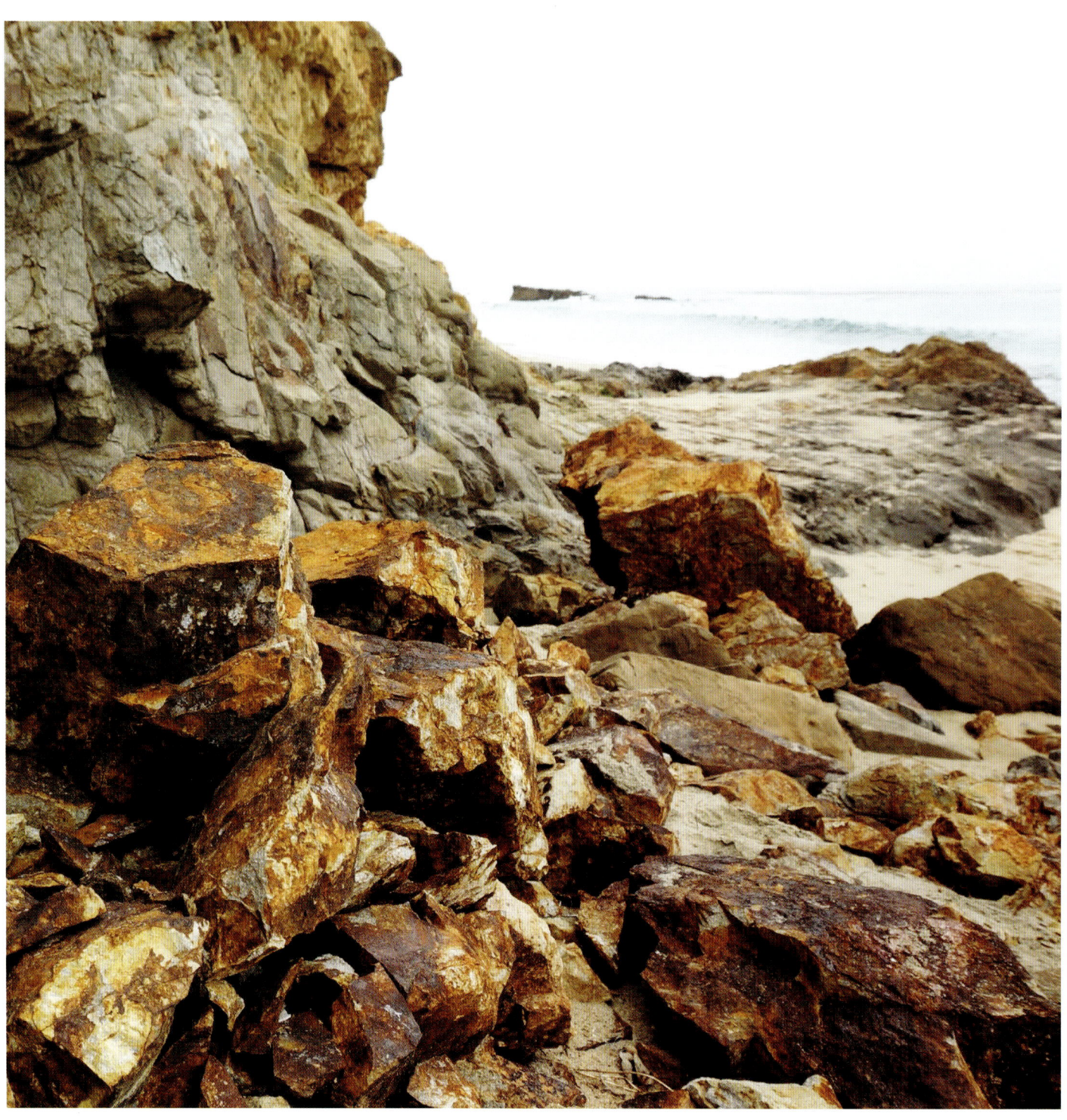

Monterey Formation, As Seen at Crystal Cove

Roughly layered rock
tells time in shades of
chalk-grey, sand and rust.

Crystal Cove

Area Closed
says the sign on the fence
enclosing a cluster of abandoned cottages—
oversized dollhouses, if you squint.

The tiny, faded shacks lean at odd angles,
missing pieces of roof here
and chunks of deck there,
like broken toys, dropped from a high place.

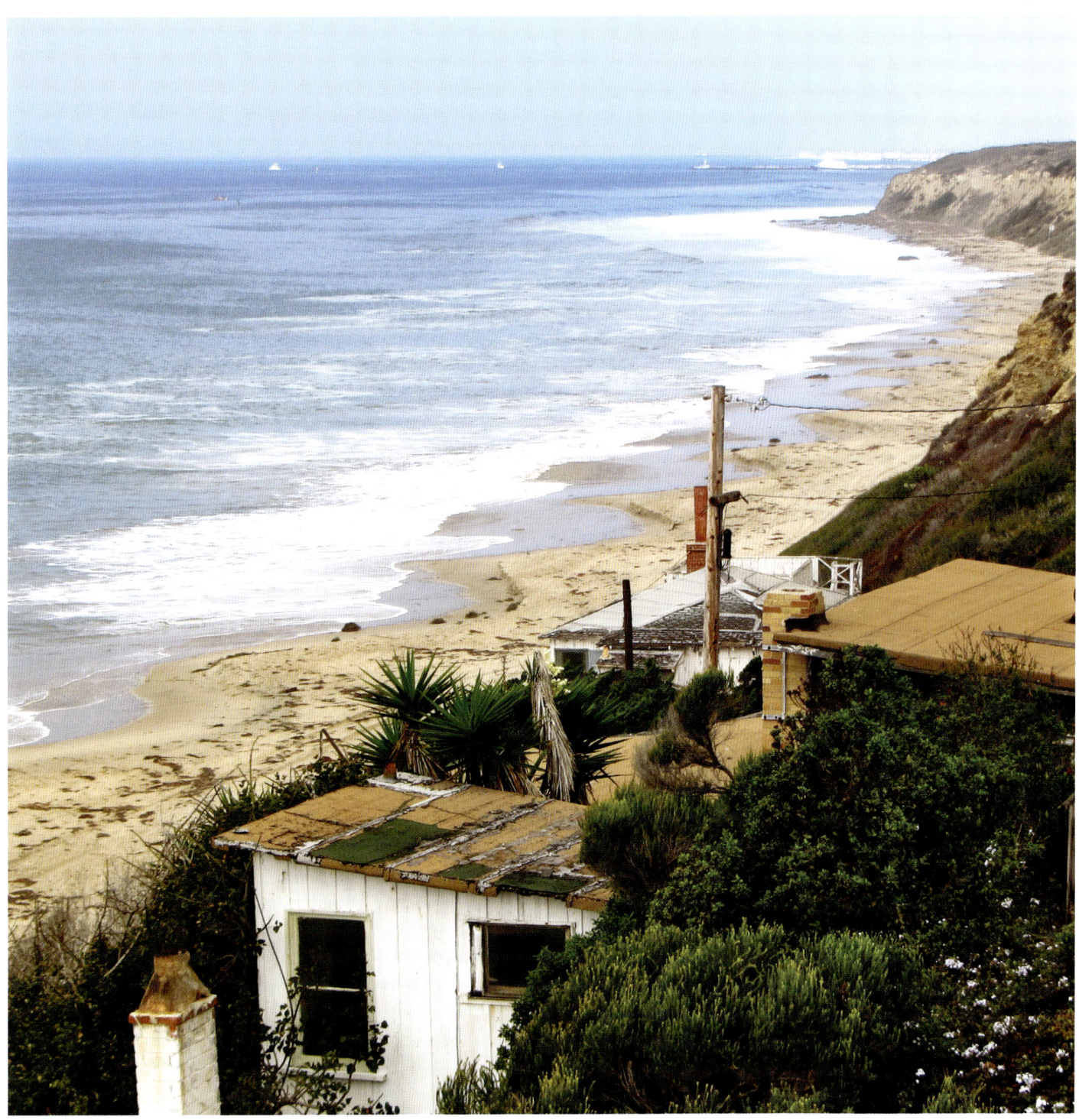

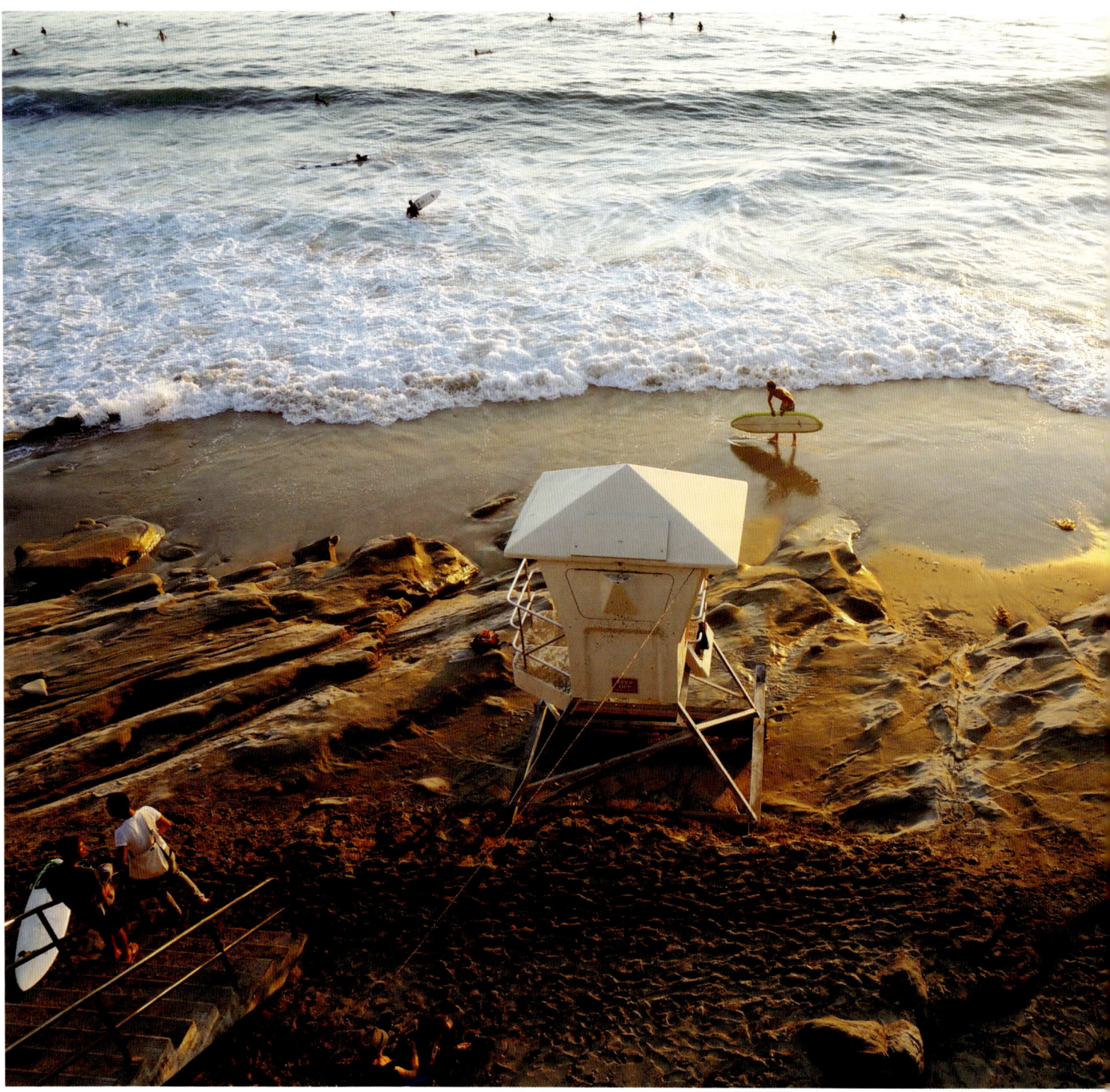

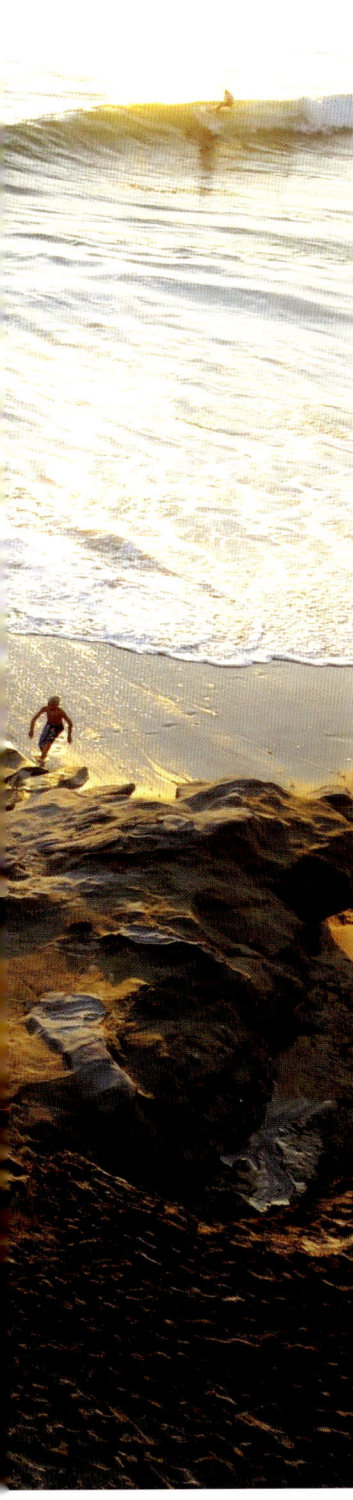

A Book At The Beach

A book at the beach.
The sound of children at play.
Lazy summer's end.

ACKNOWLEDGMENTS

Thanks to the main men in my life, David, Schuyler and Willem Vanderveen, for filling my days with love and fun. I owe a great debt of gratitude to Jennifer Anderson, a dear friend and fellow writer, without whose encouragement this book would not exist. And many thanks to my parents, Delianne and Barry Koops, for, well, everything.

Thanks to Allison Tosti for her keen designer's eye and unflagging enthusiasm for this project.

My humble and heartfelt thanks to John Van Hamersveld for allowing me to use his photograph of Rick Griffin on page 23, and to Alida Post for facilitating it.

Thanks to JoePhoto (www.joephoto.com) for permission to use his image of Cowboy on page 18. Thanks also to the Laguna Beach Independent for permission to use excerpts from Cowboy's obituary.

Thanks to Scott Sporleder (www.scottsporleder.com) for letting me use the sunrise image on pages 72-73.

Cover image provided by David Vanderveen—thanks again, honey.